Dr. Am l Jauvin

THE BOY WITH A BAMBOO HEART

he story of a street orphan who
built a children's charity

The Boy With A Bamboo Heart
First published in 2015 by Maverick House Publishers,
47 Harrington Street, Dublin 8, Ireland.

www.maverickhouse.com

email: info@maverickhouse.com

ISBN: 978-1-908518-22-4

Copyright for text © Chantal Jauvin

5 4 3 2 1

A CIP catalogue record for this book is available from the
British Library.

For Dr. Amporn, the FORDEC children, my husband Bill Thomas and my mother. Also in memory of my grand-maman and of my mentor Willis McLeese.

AUTHOR'S NOTE

YOK TUGS at my hand. She wants me to walk faster. I speak no Thai, so we smile at one another. She looks into my eyes. Hers are sunken. Her skin is translucent. With a girlish laugh, she points ahead and tells me something I do not understand. Julie translates for me. "It's her home. She has never shown it to a *farang* (foreigner) before." Nun grabs my other hand and pulls me in a different direction. She also wants to show me her home.

For an hour, the children march me through this Bangkok slum. Balancing on planks of rotting wood atop sprawling garbage, I am followed by a thread of faded red-and-white and blue-and-white uniforms. Bamboo poles support tin roofs. Sometimes blue tarps cover wood or broken concrete slabs mere inches above the trash. Petrified plastic bags, rusted scooter parts, broken pails, and spoiled vegetables litter the neighborhood.

Back at the FORDEC Day-Care Center, over green curry and rice, Dr. Amporn asks if I will help him write his story. We met through my fiancé (now husband), Bill Thomas, who has supported FORDEC for years. When he hears that I am an attorney, Dr. Amporn says, "You must speak good English and know how to write."

Before they bring the mango sticky rice for dessert, Dr. Amporn and I have agreed that I will write his life. Looking over my shoulder at Yok and Nun, who play with all the vigor of well-fed children, I know his story has to be told.

After lunch that day in March of 2010, I revisited Thailand many times to perform hundreds of hours of interviews and research before the book could take shape. First, I had to find his voice. With great patience, in person and across the ocean, he shared his life with me. In time, he trusted me with the painful details of his years in the jungle and the joys of his relationship with Father Bonningue. He remembered, sometimes with tears, what he had long buried. His sole purpose in baring his soul, as he told me many times, is to give hope to others.

My goal was to tell his story as truthfully as I could, and take the reader on the journey of his extraordinary life. Throughout my years of research and writing, his story inspired me. Where necessary, I've created dialogue, embellished descriptions, and filled in gaps of memory and research. Dr. A, as I affectionately have come to call him, has read the manuscript in its various incarnations. He confirms that I captured the essence of events, people, and places.

Writing this book has been as much of a fortunate discovery as a challenge. I had to leave behind my prism of an educated woman brought up in modern Canada with French as a mother tongue. I had to acquire the skin of an orphan who begged for his food, carried and used a rifle as a boy, took the vows of a monk, and dedicated himself to social work. If travel provides the launchpad for discovery, writing another person's life is nothing less than an exploration of one's own perspectives and views. In telling this story, I hope to have successfully captured the life of a man who had the courage to survive and thrive against tremendous odds and define for himself what belonging really means.

Chantal Jauvin
Philadelphia, Pennsylvania
July 2014

CHAPTER ONE

Ban Sawai Jeek, 1941

MY MOTHER slipped away in the middle of the night without saying good-bye. Life trickled out of her over a period of three days and then she was gone. It was an illness that even the herb man could not cure. I loved my mother. She had nicknamed me "Lek", the little one. She was the only one I had left. My father had died the previous year. I had no brothers or sisters. Like a tsunami, her death turned everything in my life upside down. I was hurled out into the world, all alone, and I was only 5 years old.

I remember the day of her funeral. The sun penetrated through the cracks in the bamboo wall of our hut. Bright light forced its way into my dark world. I turned my back on it. I wanted dawn to go away. The door creaked open. I pretended to be asleep. The nightmare that became my life had arrived in broad daylight.

Two villagers stepped into our hut. It was nothing more than one big room where everything happened—eating, mending, singing, and sleeping. The other things like cooking, cleaning, and bathing took place outside. My mother and I had shared one mattress — my favorite place — and one stool. My father's scraggly straw hat had continued to hang on a hook by the door long after he had died. My mother had refused to give it away.

One of the villagers, missing a front tooth, squatted next to me where I lay, beside my dead mother. He put his crusty hand on my shoulder and rolled me away from her body.

"Lek, little boy, it be time to take your mommy. She go to other life now." Gently, he released my fingers grasping her stiff hand. "Give you mommy a last kiss," he said.

With all my strength, I reached out to embrace her. I crushed the jasmine flowers that were still in her hair. My tears tumbled onto the sheet and onto the tattered green sarong covering her. I began to shake uncontrollably next to her lifeless body. Silently, I wished for her arms to comfort me but I knew she would never hug me again.

The hand on my shoulder tugged me away from her. Crouched on the mattress, I watched the two villagers move my mother onto our wooden cart. This was the only thing we owned. They took her out through the front door. I did not know then that this was contrary to local traditions. Corpses should be taken through a window, a roof opening or any way other than how a person normally enters the house. If not, it is believed the person is not dead and their soul will return as a ghost.

If I had had an uncle or aunt, they would have made sure to observe the proper rituals. But we had no relatives here in the village. My parents had moved here when I was only 2 years old. I had never met any of our family and did not know if they even existed.

The villagers lowered my mother onto the cart and covered her. The older man reached for my hand. On my short legs, I struggled to catch his hand and stumbled on the door ledge. No one was there to catch me. I felt the urge to run back into the house and lie down on the mattress. But my feet, heavy as sacks of rice, would not move. I began to cry, tears gushing down with enough force to fill a paddy field.

Suddenly, I stopped. I remembered how my mother had whispered to me on the day of my father's funeral.

"Lek, my sweet little one, do not sob. You must not show your emotions at a funeral. Tonight I will sing you to sleep and you can cry all you want."

The villager's hand remained outstretched, waiting for me. I wiped my tears with the back of my hand. I could not let my mother go alone. I walked up to the cart, reached for her hand, and held it tight. The men pushed the cart forward.

The sound of shuffling sandals moved toward the temple. A few family friends and some curious neighbors followed. We walked in silence. The chimes, gongs, and trumpets that were normally heard to banish the sorrows and fears of the dead were missing. The incomplete funeral procession marched on like a beheaded parade. No one walked ahead with a white banner on a long pole. No elders carried the traditional silver bowl of flowers. No monks accompanied the coffin. The only vigil for my mother had been the hours I had spent with her on the night she died. Frightened by her stillness, I had pressed against her, pretending she had just fallen asleep. I drew make-believe animals and flowers on the sarong that covered her body. I had traced the outline of her hand and sung her lullabies to help her sleep.

Unable to keep up with the cart, I skipped alongside, sometimes jerking my mother's hand, but unwilling to let it go. When I saw the pyre appear ahead of us, panic seized me. My feet dug into the ground, causing my mother's body to slip backward on the cart. The villager pulling the cart stopped and turned around to see what had happened. Without saying a word, he nodded and motioned me to keep walking.

With my gaze fixed to the ground, I took smaller steps. We stopped outside the temple grounds. Four monks waited in front of a table, which rested on a pile of wood, branches, and planks. This was not a proper cremation. It was not like my father's funeral. Why were there so few monks? Why were we not taking her inside the temple ground to the village pyre? I wondered how my mother's soul would travel safely to her next life without a real funeral.

As villagers arrived, they stayed back. They were present, yet they were absent. They did not know how to participate in this funeral that lacked the traditional rituals. No food had been offered to the monks to assist my mother's soul in traveling to her next life. No white thread joined the monks to the coffin made of old bed sheets and sarongs. The thread was necessary to carry the monks' *sutra* to my mother's body. I heard an elder say that without merit and proper rites, my mother would have a perilous journey to rebirth.

People continued to arrive from the paddy fields. Most of them were women and children. A mother in bare feet wiped her hands on an old apron and fidgeted with the handkerchief covering her hair. At her side, a little girl grinned and tugged at her mother's skirt. I remember watching the child balance on one foot, then scratching her bare leg with the toes of her free foot. A white-haired woman in a sun-faded sarong leaned on a stick. Her hands were covered with enormous callouses. She squinted and allowed her head to droop. Her smile disappeared into sorrow.

A hand yanked at my shoulder and pulled me away from my mother. I looked up and peered into the dark brown eyes of the villager.

"Come, Lek, it be time they start now."

I clutched my mother's hand, bit my bottom lip, forcing the tears to stop. I refused to cry at her funeral. I held her hand for the last time. I gave it a squeeze before releasing my grip. I was left with nothing to hold onto, not even *nat* leaves used to keep ghosts away. I tucked my trembling hands between my stomach and the rolled edge of my sarong. My chin dropped to my chest. I did not want to look at anyone, or see anyone looking at me.

The villagers who had pulled and pushed the cart from our hut then approached my mother's body.

They lifted her by the shoulders and feet to move her onto the pyre. Someone I did not recognize placed a few jasmine blossoms next to her body, a small gesture to adorn her final resting place.

One of the monks then leaned forward and placed dried bamboo shoots on each corner of the table. He set the first bunch on fire. The other three monks repeated the same actions. I did not want to see what would come next, but I could not take my eyes off my mother's body. I dug my nails deeper and deeper into the soft flesh of my stomach and bit my tongue harder. I felt no pain. It gave me courage to keep looking.

When the last monk had lit his bunch of bamboos shoots, I looked around to see what the other people were doing. Everyone was watching the fire without moving or talking. They had never seen a body cremated in this way. The flames licked the table and crept toward my mother's body. I stopped breathing. The flames joined hands, turning the sheets and sarong into a curtain of fire. A faint smell of jasmine rose from the burning flowers.

I turned away as pain exploded in my belly. I tried to scream and call for help but the words would not come out. I tried to call for her. Still nothing came out. The pain inside me had robbed me of my voice.

I forced myself to look at my mother so I could see her one last time. The flames consumed her. The sounds of burning wood and popping bamboo thundered in my head. It sounded just as scary as when she had screamed in the middle of the night in agony from her illness.

I covered my ears and howled. This time my voice rose above the burning fire. As I looked around for help, people looked away. They turned their eyes to stare at the monks. I stamped my feet and beat my fists against my thighs to get their attention. I was not crying, I was hollering.

No one moved. I stepped towards the fire. I was determined to hold her hand again. I needed to touch her one last time. The heat scorched my forehead. An old villager reached over and pulled me back, without tenderness, without anger.

I dug my toes into the ground. I refused to back away from the fire. I could not let my mother begin her journey to the other life like this. She at least had to know that I was with her. The fire that was consuming my mother's body was also searing loneliness into my heart. I stood my ground while the flames destroyed the last of any affection and tenderness I would know for the rest of my life. My mother was gone. How could I continue to exist?

As I watched on, my mother's torso suddenly shot up for a brief moment. It looked as if she was reaching out for me. I jumped back in shocked surprise. Then I moved towards her.

"I am here, Mommy," I screamed. Sweat, mixed with tears and soot, poured down my face. The urgent need to give her something to take into her next life swept over me. I had to give her something to remember me by. She could not forget me.

I ran through the small crowd towards the temple grounds. I grabbed a violet orchid and raced back to the fire. I approached the fire as close as I could stand the heat and offered her the flower. Eyes closed, I begged the universe to let her be reborn as a beautiful butterfly, like the ones she loved so much. *Most of all, please let her not forget me.*

CHAPTER TWO

AFTER THE monks and villagers left, I collapsed onto the ground and stared at the smoldering embers. One of the local women tried to coax me to go with her but I refused. She tried her best to comfort me, but she was not my mother. Eventually she gave up and walked away. I was now alone in the world — and I wanted to be left alone.

Clutching my knees, I rocked back and forth. The tears I had fought so hard to stop from flowing were gone. *Who will smile at me every morning? Who will tell me stories every night?* As I looked at the path leading back to the huts, anger swelled inside me. This village held nothing for me but bad luck. My father had died here. And now my mother was gone. No one cared if I lived or died. I wanted to leave this place and never see it again. Ever.

***

I sneaked past two old ladies who sold bananas at the edge of the village. I sneered to myself. They had no reason to care where I was going. By the time I reached the train stop, my legs ached and my stomach growled. A few minutes later, the train arrived. People stepped out of the first three train wagons to buy some noodles. A man wearing a green uniform puffing a cigarette checked the passengers' tickets.

I had never been on a train before and had no idea where it was going. It did not matter. My only desire was to escape the memories of my mother and the pity in the villagers' eyes. Without a family, I was nobody.

People boarded the first two wagons while the uniformed man disappeared to the front of the train. I headed for the last wagon where I squeezed my body through an opening the size of three bamboo trunks.

The wagon smelled of urine mixed with wet grass and dirt. Although I could not see, I realized at once this was the animal cart. A water buffalo snorted in the dark. The stench choked me and I coughed. As my eyes adjusted, I saw that metal bars restrained the beasts to one end. I crawled to the other side and hid in a dank pile of hay.

Through the opening, I saw the uniform man approaching. I froze. The door banged shut and the latch clicked into place. When the train started to move, I crept out of my hiding spot. Feeling safe for that moment, I fell asleep to the rocking motion of the train.

I woke up when the train jerked to a stop. Fearful that I would be caught, I decided to get off. Once more I squeezed through the narrow hole and slipped into the sea of people on the platform. Wherever I was, it would be my new home.

***

"Move boy. What are you doing here? Go. Go. I better not catch you in my stall again, you hear? This is not your home."

The man shouted at me. I scurried to my feet, grabbed my sandals and ran. I felt the sting of a bamboo pole thrashing at my legs. *How come I had not heard the morning sounds?* Usually, the vendors' squeaky carts woke me, providing enough warning for me to disappear before they reached their stalls. Not this morning. The owner caught me sleeping under his fruit table. More bad luck.

I scolded myself. This was the best place I had found to sleep for weeks. The new merchant had installed fresh wooden planks to display his produce, which gave me some protection. He was hardworking and cleaned his stall every night. *Stupid boy.* I cursed myself under my breath again. I zigzagged through the rickety stands avoiding the rotten jackfruits, chicken bones and scraps of dried squid festering on the ground.

When I reached the road, I slowed down. I would have to sleep in the open until I found a new spot. A few months before, I had found a hideout on the outskirts of town which I returned to when I had nowhere else to go. A bunch of *kalamona* trees, thick with yellow blossoms, provided me with some shelter. It was not perfect, but it would have to do. People call the flowers "scrambled eggs" because of the way they clung together. People joked that they could not be eaten. I tried once and vomited throughout the night.

To pass the time, I washed my sarong and my hair in the runoff from the paddy fields. My mother had taught me how important it was to keep myself clean. Without a home, and with no water, I often resorted to scrubbing dirt off my body with ashes from the market.

An old lady showed me how to clean my teeth. Every day, she sat on a cinder block by the side of the road, her legs bent to the side and her bare feet sticking out, as if waiting for something. And every day she wore the same faded blue cotton blouse and a pair of beige fisherman's pants tied around her toothpick-sized waist. She gazed into the empty fields as if she was watching a joyful parade of days gone by. She never uttered a word. I had no idea how old she was. I had rarely seen such white hair.

One day as I was walking back to my hideout, she raised her arm and waved me over. Startled, I approached her slowly, ready to dart off at any moment. I could not figure out whether she really wanted me to come closer or if she was in another place, in another time. Her eyes and nose hid behind many wrinkles. Her brilliant white teeth seemed to belong to a different face. She extended a hand and offered me a few shriveled leaves.

"Here, little one," she said.

"These are leaves from my toothbrush tree. Scrub these against your teeth every day and you will keep them shiny as the stars. You see, Mother Nature gives us all we need."

I saw her from time to time after that but she never spoke to me again.

***

Pain was the only constant in my life. Loneliness, shame and fear consumed me. I could never soothe the burning ache inside. I had temporary reprieves from misery however. Sometimes I overcame my disgust with stray dogs. They reminded me too much of myself. Sometimes I would befriend one, curling up with him at night for warmth. Hunger worked the same way. When I was sufficiently hungry, I could set aside the goodness my mother had instilled in me and steal.

Saturdays were the best day for stealing. I wandered the marketplace and eyed the fleshy mangoes, jackfruits and rose apples. Fruits were my favorite things to eat. I stayed away from the fried chicken, sticky rice and noodles. Even if I spent half my time dreaming about these delicacies, cooked foods were out of reach. I could not pocket them without making a mess or getting caught.

I walked to the center of the stalls, brushing past steaming woks of fried pork noodles, scrambled eggs and boiling pots of fish ball soup. I looked for the busiest parts of the market and avoided stealing from the same vendor twice in a row.

The market was filled with rows of wobbly, weather-worn crates which bulged with fruits and vegetables.

For shade, the more industrious vendors, or those who could afford to, hung corrugated tin sheets on bamboo poles. This created the perfect obstacle course for adults and allowed me to scamper through more easily. Rusty carts and barrels filled with dried squid, fish and pork comprised the next section. I stayed away from meat and fish because I had nowhere to cook. But even if I did, I had no idea how to cook. The poorer farmers laid their crops on banana or palm leaves on the ground. I was not quite desperate enough to steal from them.

I would look for a vendor surrounded by buyers reaching for produce and vying for his attention. I pretended to play with a stick and stone before making a move. If I saw a villager carrying a parcel, I would bump into her. In the commotion, I would grab something and run. Sometimes someone would chase me. But most of the time, the person would not realize I had robbed them until it was too late.

Once safely out of view, I would find a place to examine my loot. I usually ended up with a few cucumbers and tomatoes. Sometimes I got lucky; at other times, I was not so lucky. Sometimes I would discover that I had stolen onions and garlic.

***

I can still recall occasional acts of kindness. One of the meat sellers who had never caught me stealing would sometimes offer me food she was about to discard.

"Here dark boy, I just cleaned out some chickens. You can have the guts. If you go to the edge of the market, the old man is burning rubbish. Maybe he'll let you cook them."

She wrapped the bloody mess in a palm leaf and handed it to me. I reached for it, but my vision was blurry and the gift thumped to the ground.

"What's wrong with you boy? You don't want it?"

"Yes, Ma'am, I do want it very much. I'm very sorry. I don't see so well in the last few days. I think I'm going blind."

I bent over and picked up the bag.

"You can't be going blind. You're too young, boy. Come over here."

I hesitated, clutching the bundle as I approached her. I was not about to give it back.

She looked into my eyes, waved her hand around and told me to follow it. I just stared back at her. She put her hand on my forehead. I stiffened. I felt her rough skin as her hand moved toward my cheek. No one had touched me for a long time.

"You're warm boy. Maybe you're sick?"

"No Ma'am, just hungry. I've been throwing up the last two weeks. Maybe it's from something I ate from the garbage pile."

I stepped away from her while guarding the chicken guts.

"You know the *neem* tree?" she asked.

"No Ma'am."

"It's the one that has branches with long leaves. The bark is little bit red."

"Yes, the one that has really bitter leaves?"

"Yes. Chew these leaves every day. It will kill any bugs in your stomach. Maybe you ate food that had bugs in it and now they are in your belly. It also helps with your eyes."

She looked into the distance.

"Maybe you have the sickness."

"What sickness?"

"Deadly Malla. You know ma-la-ria. My father died from it," she said.

"What's that?"

I became frightened. I remembered my mother yelling with pain, clutching her stomach in the middle of the night. Was that what she had died of? I pushed the question out of my mind.

"It's a bad sickness. You can't see at night. You have fever, throw up, and there is blood when you go pee. If you don't take medicine for it, you die."

"I don't have money for medicine," I said.

I reached for her hand, forced her to look at me and asked with a trembling voice, "Am I going to die?"

"I don't know if you have the sickness. Just chew lots of *neem* leaves. Now go. Leave me alone. I must get home."

Terrified, I walked over to the old man burning garbage to ask him if I could cook the guts on his fire. When he spoke to me, I did not respond. I did not want anybody to know if I had the disease. I was afraid the villagers would send me away. This town had been my home for five years. I did not want to leave. Then I wondered. *If you die from being sick, maybe you have*

*better life next life. Maybe I won't get punished for all
my stealing. Maybe I won't come back as a worm.*

"What you thinking boy?" asked the old man,
interrupting my thoughts. He chewed his words in the
same way he chewed his *paan*. I did not understand
why old people chewed this mix of areca nut and betel
leaves. I tried it once, when I was starving. It tasted
awful, like sucking on a piece of soap.

I did not know if I should ask him. I was afraid he
would find out I was sick and tell the other villagers.
But who else could I ask? I had to know. Maybe I
should not chew the *neem* leaves to get better. Maybe
I should just take a chance.

"If someone dies because they are sick, do they get a
better second life?" I blurted.

"I don't know, boy. Why do you ask me? I guess it
depends on what that person did before they died.
Were they a good person or a bad person?"

I did not like his answer. I knew I was a bad boy.

***

My body shivered from the rain and my stomach
growled endlessly. I had not eaten in days. Everything
was soggy. The market was too empty to attempt
stealing anything. I stared at the raindrops falling into
an old bamboo cup. I distracted myself by dreaming of
a big brother, of not being alone. But I dared not think
of my mother. My stomach cramps worsened. I often
cried with the pain. I had promised myself I would
not beg, but I was past caring about my shame.

I wobbled to the market. I had to do it; I had to eat. I approached the noodle stands where a young couple were laughing over a bowl of steaming soup. They seemed immune to the cold. The smell of boiling broth, pork and kaffir leaves hit me hard. I dropped my head, averted my eyes to the ground and raised my hands above my head in the familiar gesture of a beggar. With tears running down my face, I forced the words out:

"Kind persons, I beg you. Please give me something to eat. I am so hungry."

The young man, visibly angered by my interruption, slapped the back of my lowered head.

"Tell your parents to feed you then."

I braced myself for another slap but asked again.

"Please, sir. I have no parents. I am so cold and hungry. I haven't eaten in days."

The cook standing by the boiling pot shoved me to the ground.

"Go, dark boy. You are bothering my clients. Go now."

I picked myself up and staggered away. I dropped to the ground behind an empty stall. I could not take my eyes off the young couple. They were laughing with the cook as they said good-bye. Shame burned inside me. Then it hardened into anger. All I wanted was some leftovers, what their full bellies would leave behind.

My rage gave me strength. I dragged myself to my feet and walked to the table with the two half-finished soup bowls. My stomach demanded to be fed. My mouth watered, I could taste the salty soup and I could feel the hot liquid warming me as it relieved my hunger. Just as I reached the table, the cook stepped in front of the table. He grabbed the bowls and tossed the leftover noodles to the ground.

"Go, boy. There is nothing for you here. Unless you're like a dog, then go ahead, lick the noodles off the ground."

I stared at the noodles and bits of pork. Just as I started to reach down for them, the cook squished the noodles into the wet ground with his sandals.

"Don't you dare come back here dark boy and disturb my customers. You hear?"

CHAPTER THREE

IT WAS like any other day, a battle to survive. But that day would lead to an entirely different kind of fighting. I sat at the edge of the market by the food stalls waiting to pounce on any noodles customers might leave unfinished. Two men talked over steaming bowls of pork ball soup. I observed their every move. I positioned myself closer, ready to hustle if any scraps were left. The men leaned in and spoke softly. One looked like a local — ordinary, with a nervous smile. The other one did most of the talking. He covered his mouth with his right hand. The dark sunglasses and green cap framed his high forehead. He wore laced boots and a matching black leather belt. A flashlight, satchel, and hooks hung from the belt. His jaw relaxed as he chewed a toothpick. He held himself with an air of authority, which was unfamiliar in these parts. I overheard bits and pieces of their conversation.

"You make lotta money. They hirin' any boys willin' to sweat in the jungle and ..." The sentence trailed off.

"Where they takin' the boys?" asked the one doing most of the listening.

"Kampuchea. You see, the Kampucheans, they need to get rid of them French soldiers. They don't got enough men or guns. Some smart Thai has been gettin' Thai boys to go fight. They pay 'em OK money. The French, they know nothing' about fightin' in the jungle. So no big risk …"

I heard the last part about "OK money." I lost my interest in the soup. I moved closer.

The man with the sunglasses spotted me. He snapped, "You listenin' to us?"

"No," I answered. "But how old do you got to be? To get work in the jungle?"

"You old enough boy. You interested?"

I nodded.

"Come see me in the morning. Be ready, because we head out early."

When I walked away, he called out, "You got family?"

I shook my head. A faint smile appeared on his face. I wondered why.

The days and nights that followed muddled into one another. The next morning, they transported us in the back of a pickup truck farther from home than I had ever been. The roads snaked into small trails. The villages became more scattered. Then we penetrated the woods. There were five of us. We peered at each other, unwilling to be the first to talk. The other four were bigger than me. They looked stronger, too. What was obvious — our shared poverty. Maybe their families forced them to come. They appeared to be around my age.

I worked hard to keep a smile off my face and hide my desperation. All I cared about was earning money. I wanted to buy food, not steal it, to eat each day, maybe even twice a day. I could no longer recall my mother's face. I no longer saw her eyes searching mine, questioning what I was doing. She was gone from my soul. Without her, I had lost my last bit of dignity. Without a friend or elder to fill some of the void, to see me, I had stopped existing. I was nobody.

I leaned back against the rusted cab of the pickup and tucked my knees to my chest to avoid touching the other boys. I fell asleep to the jerks and bumps, without giving a thought to what I would be doing in the jungle. I figured if they were hiring poor boys like us, the work had to be hard. I was ready to do anything.

When I woke from my nap, the truck had stopped. We had arrived at our destination. They herded us off to a grassy area, where another 15 Thai boys joined us. I imagined they arrived under similar circumstances. I leered at them. Disheveled, hungry and weary, we were nothing but an unhinged bunch. I detected the same fear and anxiety in their faces.

Within minutes, it began. In choppy sentences our leaders told us we would be trained in jungle warfare. I had no idea what that meant. They lined us up by height. One of the smaller uniformed men shoved me to the short end of the line. Another barked at us to face forward and start running. My boy soldier training had begun.

At first, it felt good to be told what to do. Nothing, not the dank underbrush, mosquitos or tiring runs dampened my spirit. The break of dawn was met each morning with a bowl of plain clumpy rice. They did not even bother to warm it up. Every night I flopped onto a straw mat too exhausted to think about what was happening. We shared a couple of makeshift open-air cottages. The boys outnumbered the hammocks. Most fought to get one, I did not care. I was happy with the floor. It was better than most anywhere I had slept for the last 10 years.

We kept to ourselves, eyeballing each other and gawking at anyone in uniform. A sense of foreboding saturated the air. The rainy season with its cyclones was fast approaching. The air was heavy with moisture and bugs. The first storm was about to strike at any moment.

A Cambodian man dressed in army fatigues shouted at us in Khmer day and night. Khmer was spoken in the small villages where they had picked us up. I understood most of it. The "Commandant" made a pig butcher look harmless. Everything about him suggested violence, indifference, and authority. When he removed his cap, a scar from botched-up stitches revealed an unnatural gap between his cheek and right ear. His appearance terrified me. I looked past him and thought of the money I was about to earn. His features were foreign to me. I told myself that the minute I had enough money, I would quit and leave. Already, I never wanted to see his face again.

The Commandant made us run around paddy fields a few times a day. That I did not mind. But I hated the other drills. We had to slide on our stomachs, and squirm back and forth to squeeze under brush and wires. Our chins were forced below the foul waterline. The drillmaster praised the boys who wriggled like water snakes. I was not one of them. My skin itched from the filth and I was bloated like a frog. But I kept trying harder. I yearned for the same recognition. I became obsessed with a need for their praise.

My resentment was brewing, especially during midday meals. They gave each of us a bowl of steaming noodles. If we failed to return an empty bowl within five minutes, one of the Commandant's underlings kicked the bowl from our hands. It splattered onto the ground. This made me furious. Why were they wasting all this food?

The first time it happened, I reached, out of habit, for the noodles on the ground. The soldier stepped on them with his muddy boots. Then he sneered at me.

"You eat fast o' you don't eat. It's no fuckin' family dinner. In the jungle, you quick at everythin' o' you die." The sight of the spoiled noodles triggered rage within me that I dared not let it out.

After the first week, the stronger boys became cocky. A pecking order emerged for bullying rights. Being among the youngest, I was near the top for receiving and near the bottom for giving.

The training soldiers woke us in the middle of the night more frequently as the weeks moved on. We stumbled out of our hammocks or fumbled to our feet from the mats. They pointed flashlights into our eyes and barked conflicting commands.

"Lie down. Run. Jump to your feet. Don't move. Hands in the air."

We froze, unable to figure out which order to obey. The men kicked our knees, sending us to the ground. Bullies received extra body blows, which they later passed onto us weaker boys in revenge.

One such night, I reacted too slowly to the warning. Not yet on my feet, I felt the soldier hissing above me.

"Dead. You're a dead boy."

Eyes bulging, he spat at me. He made sure I understood who was in charge.

"You're a dead boy," he repeated.

Before I had a chance to protect myself, he raised his gun with both hands and drove the butt end into the soft flesh of my side.

Pain exploded in my ribs. My vision blurred. I saw fiery colors for an instant and then everything went black. Wheezing and flopping about on the ground, I waited for the next blow. Should I fight back? Was this the lesson? The agony blocked my ability to think. Curled up in a ball, I braced for the next assault.

"Ha-ha-ha. Look at you now, boy. You little scared shit. You won't last a day out there in the jungle." With a half-sneer, half-laugh, he walked away.

We tried to hide our fear. We stayed awake the rest of the night nursing our wounds, waiting for the next raid. Anger overtook humiliation, and hate settled in.

After that night, we slept in our clothes. Sometimes we had three or four raids a night. At the first sound of approaching boots, we warned each other. We took the abuse and never fought back. Wound up tighter and tighter, we stored up reserves of violence. We knew that someday, on command, we would unleash savagery against an adversary chosen for us.

In the mornings, after a quick bowl of soup, we were forced into swamps until our bruised bodies bloated into sun-seared chilies. Other days, we had to climb trees, hide in the branches, and wait quietly. We attackers were told to listen for "woo-ta-woo," a high-pitched birdcall. The signal might come in a few minutes — or hours. Straining to hear it nearly drove us crazy. When it came, we were instructed to jump the shirtless boys and peg them until they were unable to move. If a boy got away, the attackers were punished for letting him escape. They forced us to climb a tree and jump down until we dropped of fatigue while the shirtless heroes hurled insults at us.

When I had to stay awake for a long time or contain my anger, I forced myself to count the coins I received each week. Then I repeated my survival chant.

When I get enough money, I'll leave. I'll go to a new village, find a nice girl, and marry her. I'll be a man and a father. I'll bury my past so deep no one will ever know about it.

I had no idea where we were other than a vague awareness that Surin was about a three hour jeep ride from this hell. It did not matter, I was not going back there.

Because I did not know how to read and write, I was in the lowest rank. The soldiers ridiculed us. The boys who were barely literate mimicked them: "If you no read, you no better than a dog." The soldiers placed our food on the ground. The bullies barked and growled to further antagonize us. The leaders wanted to break us. We weak boys did everything we could to be on their side but it was futile. The humiliation was worse than the bruises and verbal assaults. The words echoed in my ears for days.

The helplessness and dejection I felt from years of living on the streets mixed with this abuse fermented into anger of the worst kind. I lived to insult and assault the other boys. I craved the soldiers' praise. I learned how vile my tongue could be.

"Maybe I can't read, but my mom is no fucking prostitute like yours," I yelled. "Sure, I can't write my name, but you can't count the number of goddamn brothers and sisters you have."

With each abasement I suffered, I searched for another put-down to hurl at them. My fury and hatred fueled and justified my verbal assaults. The nameless boy I had been when I arrived from Surin was dead, suffocated by this tormented place. In his place emerged a repulsive thug willing to do anything — anything — to win his captives' favor. I had long ago stopped trying to please my mother. I had buried every thought and image of her. I no longer cared about reincarnation. I wanted to become one of the soldiers, to get glory in this life. To hell with what came next.

The pace accelerated after the first month. The Commandant said the Kampucheans needed men, and soon. The Commandant and his men huddled closer together at mealtimes. In the evening, their drinking escalated. We barely slept. They began calling us over, forcing us to drink thick liquor. At first we got sick. In time, we learned that it helped us forget and made us braver. So we begged for a swig whenever they took out their bottles. They made us wrestle for their enjoyment. The winner got a mouthful of liquor. The soldiers' cheers and drunken pats on the back were equally intoxicating. They made cockfighters out of us. In the days and weeks that followed, they wound us up tighter and tighter. As the soldiers drank more, they became more ferocious in their training techniques and their punishments. Boys bullied other boys. They began tasting pleasure when they inflicted pain on a weaker boy. I experienced the rush of exacting suffering, of being the enforcer instead of the victim. I enjoyed it. The soldiers bet on which of us would kill first. This fed our bravado. We punched harder, kicked more fiercely, and cursed even louder.

Although none of us had held a weapon, we talked tough. Our distance from reality grew. We could hardly contain our impatience to fight. The soldiers drilled anger into us and made our bodies stronger but none of us, them included, knew anything about the tactics of guerilla warfare. Fueled by pent-up energy and naïveté, we practiced ambushes like schoolboys in after-school games. We competed for the rank of toughest bully, filthiest mouth, and most indifferent halfwit. We emulated the soldiers who had become our heroes. We each had our favorite.

The men divided us into two teams; one team wore T-shirts, the other team was bare-chested. The goal was simple: to capture the opposing team. When a team lost, they were punished by the other team. Bored with insults, the winners progressed to rib punches. Heads were off-limits because we needed our sight to fight. We unleashed years of past abuse on each other, always vying to be the toughest and meanest.

The soldiers called our teams, "units." They were our band of brothers. We learned to hate and mistrust the boys from the other units. My unit had five boys. Dieng was the tallest and oldest at 17. Dom was dark-skinned, very shy, and 15. Serree was the toughest. Piak was the smallest and youngest, but the bravest and fastest. They called me "Boney." I was the skinniest and second youngest. We had no choice but to tolerate each other. If we were smart, the soldiers told us, we would learn to trust each other, as our lives might depend on it. I kept to myself. We had no idea how long we would be together or if the units would be shuffled into new groups.

The fifth week began with another midnight raid. By now, I had grown accustomed to them. As I scrambled out of my hammock, I could tell something was different. But what? I arrived out of breath at the meeting place for line-up. The Commandant stood before us holding a gun. Ten men with guns stood on either side of him. Nobody spoke. No one shouted to shut up. We had never seen more than one or two guns. This was an army. My team stood in the second row. My eyes were glued to the guns. My legs weakened. I forgot to breathe, and shoved my hands into my pockets so no one could see I was trembling. My righteousness and animosity disappeared, my baseless bravery vanished.

I asked myself if I could handle a gun.

On the Commandant's signal, the men raised their guns and took aim at us. We were no longer playing games for the soldiers' entertainment.

"Shoot!" he ordered.

We ran for cover. I dove behind an overturned coal barrel, shivering and holding back vomit. One boy lay face down in the dirt, his hands over his ears, shoulders quivering. When he glanced at me, it was not the tears in his eyes that frightened me, but his look of helplessness. No one moved. The Commandant said something that made the men laugh. I heard multiple thumps, and saw their rifle butts hit the ground, barrels pointed to the sky.

The Commandant spoke. "Boys, come back and line up."

No one dared to move.

"NOW."

His order echoed in the darkness.

Afraid to disobey, we reformed our lines.

"You boys ready. You got good survival instincts. Today you get weapons. Tomorrow we head to the jungle for real training." He whispered something to his second-in-command, and left.

I stared at the spot where he had been, a ghost foreshadowing brutality. None of us made eye contact. Fear filled the stale air. I stole a quick look and saw many wet pants.

That day, everything changed. For the first time in my life, I held a weapon in my hands. Maybe it was a test, to see who among us hesitated. The moment my finger curled around the trigger, I knew I would never be a boy again. Whatever bravery I had displayed before was borrowed.

The soldiers laughed less and drank more. We boys bullied each other less and stared into the distance more.

The Commandant reappeared mid-morning. We had never seen him twice in one day.

"Boys, this is a bayonet," he yelled. "This is your weapon. You guard it with your life."

He ordered the soldiers to detach the spiked bayonet from their rifles and hand them to us. The Commandant, standing before the fourth soldier from the left, kneeled, reached for the round metal piece at the front of the gun, and twisted it off. He stood up, saw me staring, and walked toward me.

I wanted to run but feared someone would shoot me in the back. He extended the blade to me. I had no choice. I took it. I turned it in my hands. It was longer than my arm. The pointy end was sharp. Should I hold it—firmly or gently? Was I to take charge of it, or let it take charge of me?

"You use this weapon to get yourself a gun." He paused for emphasis on "gun."

When he had the attention of all of the boys, he continued.

"You kill Frenchman, you take his gun. Then, you will be a real mercenary."

What food remained in my stomach shot up my throat. I closed my mouth to keep from vomiting. I leaned against the bayonet to support my weak legs. I had no idea what a mercenary was, but I had no desire to kill a man to find out.

"Tomorrow you will get your first chance to be real mercenary. Now go with my men for training. Remember, you must never lose this weapon. To survive in the jungle you need a gun. Bayonets are not enough."

His voice rose.

"You kill anyone not on our side. They are invaders and traitors. You hear me?"

"Yes," the soldiers shouted, holding their guns in the air.

"You hear me?" the Commandant repeated.

"Yes."

A few boys raised their bayonets in the air along with the soldiers.

"You hear me?" His face red, his eyes fierce, the Commandant raised his arms high above his head.

"Yes."

Every gun and bayonet was in the air. A mix of drunken bravery and fearful shouts were directed at the sky. The soldiers slapped our backs, inciting us to scream louder.

"Yes."

We shouted the war cry over and over.

Did they know how unprepared we were?

We spent the next morning learning to climb trees, the bayonets scraping against our backs. We held them with one hand and scaled the trees with the other. In the afternoon, the soldiers led us to a shaded area. We practiced stabbing bags of dirt, learning the best angle to inflict harm and the best hand position for pulling out the bayonet and stabbing again. Between strikes, we drank lots of water to lessen our thirst the next day.

"Kill! Kill! Kill!" we shouted with every jab.

Before the day ended, the Commandant reappeared. He carried a bucket of blood. "Cow blood", he said. He forced us one at a time to stick our hands in the bucket, and rub the blood on our hands and arms, then all over our faces.

"Tomorrow, this will be enemy blood. You must see and taste blood today, so tomorrow you thirst for it."

CHAPTER FOUR

"BONEY, GRAB the fuckin' gun and run!" yelled the soldier.

My feet were pinned to the ground. I watched the ambush roaring around me. Some boys ran. Others were falling, disappearing into the thick vegetation. Jungle cats and vultures would pounce on their sweaty flesh. I stood there silently yelling, Get up and run! They will shoot you. Run!

It was too late; they had already been shot. They were covered in their own blood, not the Commandant's cow blood nor the traitor's. This blood was gushing life out of them.

"Take the fuckin' gun and run," the soldier yelled again, and motioned to me.

I was reading his lips, trying to make sense of his words. I watched another of our soldiers ram the butt of his rifle into the forehead of a boy on the ground. Blood gurgled from his mouth. The boy struggled to his knees. He wheezed until the soldier delivered a second blow to his face. The body slumped to the ground and was still. I had seen death before, the sick dwindling kind, but this was different. Your humanity died along with them as you witnessed boys and men being slaughtered.

The soldier picked up the rifle lying on the ground, shoved it into my arms.

"What are you waiting for, dumb shit? Take this back to camp. Don't stop for anything except to kill one of them. But don't waste bullets."

He grabbed my hands and positioned the gun across my outstretched arms, the way you would carry a load of bamboo sticks. He hit me across the back of the head.

"Run back to camp, and don't stop till you get there. You done good, boy, you got yourself a gun. Now run."

The soldier whirled around, contorted his face into a cry more fearful than a tiger's and plunged his bayonet into the boy's stomach. Was this an act of hatred or kindness?

I ran toward the camp, panting, tripping over roots. I never let go of the gun. It was dark when I got to camp.

Joining the others around the campfire and fighting for air, I let the rifle thump to the ground. I looked around at the soldiers. They had the eyes of old men. I grabbed the bottle from someone's hand. Without asking, I tossed it back and drank until I began to choke. Someone pulled the bottle away.

"Slow down, boy. Boney here's had his first kill. Well done, boy. You're a soldier now. Take a bottle, you deserve it. You're one of us."

All eyes turned to me. I felt something release in my gut. I took one more mouthful. Then I spotted the dried-up blood on my hands and pants, and my stomach contracted. I retched all over my boots.

The soldiers laughed and punched one another in play.

"Boney's going to be a real bloodsucker."

I dragged myself to the cottage, threw myself on the ground and rolled under the platform. I recoiled in horror. Voices swirled in my head. I did not kill him, I only stabbed him, I had to or he would have killed Dom.

"Boney here's had his first kill."

"A soldier killed him, not me," I whispered to myself.

"I just jabbed him. No harm done. I've got to get out of here. I don't want to do this. I've got to leave in the morning, go where they won't find me, before I kill someone for real."

The next morning, I found myself standing to attention with a few other boys. I held a clean rifle in front of the Commandant. I did not recognize the weapon from the day before. In my gut I knew someone had wiped the blood off it. This was the gun. Someone had died for me to get this gun.

"You boys are the strong ones. You got a gun on your first ambush. You brave boys. You train with the soldiers to use gun. Then, when you shoot the pig invader and kill the bastards, you be real soldier."

The Commandant paused to look at each of us. When he got to me, I braced myself.

"You did good. Real good."

He poked my shoulder before moving on.

I looked down. Warmth pumped through my veins.

"You stay with soldiers. You learn to shoot a gun. When you ready, you go for first kill. You be my men."

He looked in our direction, nodding to those of us holding guns.

I felt his words travel up my spine. My chest puffed and my shoulders squared. Something had changed. We stood straighter. We were being rewired. Using praise and kinship, the Commandant was fanning the low-burning embers to set a fire ablaze.

With eight other boys, I spent the next few days repeating the same drills, but this time carrying a gun. I learned to hold it, to load five bullets into the magazine, and then jam it into the gun. Because those were all the bullets we had, we would have to steal more from the other side. This meant killing them first.

The soldiers trained us to raise the bolt handle to keep the gun from firing, then to pull it back before shooting. Except we did not shoot, we had to save the bullets for the real fight. We only practiced aiming at targets. Our accuracy would be measured by whether we returned.

The rifles were long and heavy, made of wood and steel. We tore our hands inserting and removing the bayonets. The guns were useless weapons, nothing more than sickle handles, until we had bullets. The rifle was awkward. I tried to figure out the best way to carry it. Because I was so short, when the bayonet was in place, I had to be careful to point the tip up or it would catch fallen branches and launch me backwards.

"You dead, boy."

The training soldier yelled, "Get up, get up. You fall to ground, the Frenchmen, they jump on you, they much bigger. They hit you in face, then grab your gun and stab you. You're dead and they haven't wasted a single bullet. Get up, Boney. Pick up your gun. Point that damn gun up. How many times do I gotta tell you? You lose your gun, you're dead."

No matter how tired or sore I was at the end of each day, I never skipped noodles. The broth, with morsels of who knows what, always tasted the same. Amid the turmoil, the one sure thing in my life was a bowl of food at least twice a day.

Some nights, on my way to my hammock, the soldiers amused themselves by forcing me to drink a few slurps from the bottle. The taste was vile, a fermented brew concocted for the insane. The after-effect was better than medicine. I pretended I hated it. In truth, I craved the burning that killed the thoughts running through my head. The charade also gave me a sense of belonging. I liked when they said, "Soon you be one of us, Boney." Then they would slap my shoulders, push me down the path, and drown me with their raucous, drunken slurs.

***

"Man, this waitin' stinks," I said.

"We been in this shithole for a day. I'm sick and tired of this. They ain't no enemy around here. I want to go back to camp. We missin' all the booze," I said while I poked Dieng's ribs to bug him.

We had been posted as lookouts 20 kilometers away from camp since dawn the previous day. We no longer bothered with every sound we heard.

Irritated, Dieng said, "Stop it, dumb shit. Keep watchin'. It's my turn to rest."

Dieng swatted a mosquito on his neck. He mumbled to himself, something he was doing more and more.

I hated this routine. I was so bored; I wanted action. I swiped at a mosquito on the back of Dieng's head. The booze, the waiting and the fear had transformed me into a dirty-mouthed scoundrel.

"Stop being a cow," Dieng said.

A burst of gunshots drowned out the chant of cicadas. We grabbed our guns, hands trembling, and squirmed to the front of the dugout. In the time it took us to travel a few yards, we had gone from boys to crazed, make-believe soldiers. Birds flew overhead, branches snapped, gunshots reverberated — real ones fired in our direction. We took aim at the uproar, like a couple of rabid dogs striking out. We were bush-trained street children who lacked any combat experience.

"*Général, Général, où êtes-vous?*" (General, General, where are you?) came a voice.

"*Tirez, bon sang*! (Shoot, dammit!) *Tirez!* (Shoot!)," said another.

I had no idea what was being said but I knew they were approaching, and fast. Staring straight ahead in the darkness, I ordered my finger to hold steady on the trigger. My stomach pressed against the ground, I braced my arms the way they taught us. The instant I saw a branch tremble, I pulled the trigger.

A voice cried out.

"*Merde — je suis frappé.*" (Shit — I've been hit.)

I rolled over onto my back, reloaded my gun. Dieng was doing the same.

"How many down, do you think?" Dieng asked.

"Dunno."

I remembered to spare my bullets.

"We should grab the guns and run," I said. "We don't want to be outta bullets before we get back to camp."

I was close enough to see Dieng's smile.

He sprang up and screamed. Dieng's body was hurled backward with an ear-splitting blast.

"Dieng, Dieng," I yelled while crawling over to him.

"Ah, help me. I've been hit. Damn, it hurts. Argh."

I saw blood gushing from both his legs and nothing below his knees. I grabbed a branch, stuck it into Dieng's mouth to stop his screaming. The gunfire slowed. An uneasy hush fell between the distant chaos and us. I heard brush crackling under approaching footsteps.

"Hey, brother, you be all right. Stay here. Be quiet. I'm gonna go take care of these bastards. Then you and me, we goin' back to camp, you hear me?"

Dieng shook his head, blood trickling out the side of his mouth. I put his gun back in his arms.

"Anybody comes close, you shoot him, you hear? You shoot his fuckin' brains out."

Dieng stared back at me with his eyes wide open.

"Shit. No, Dieng. No."

The rifle fire was getting closer. I had to get out of there. I ran until my lungs collapsed, robbing me of air. I dove behind a big rubber tree. Tears spilled out.

The years had toughened me up. But death, death still made me cry. At night when the golden liquid failed to numb me anymore, when the other boys had passed out, I cried.

I knew Dieng would not make it. By this stage, there was only Piak and me left. Hatred, the kind that comes from your very core and shuts your brain down exploded within me. It turned me from a calculating human being into a raging baboon. I was no longer Lek. I was a wounded animal out for a kill.

I crouched behind the tree, steadied my breath, and waited for the storm of gunshots. Raising my rifle, I waited for the goon. In this place of senseless killing, the dividing lines blurred. The battle cry erupted from a victimized Kampuchea defending itself against a French aggressor who had spilled its war with Vietnam onto their territory. I was a Thai boy shooting at North African French soldiers in a jungle somewhere in Cambodia. We were all displaced animals.

We had traded the futility of the streets for the promise of easy money. Along the way, the Commandant brainwashed us into believing we served a purpose. The soldiers on the other side were invaders and we had a right to kill them. But none of us had seen or experienced the injustices that had been perpetrated. After all the inequities we had endured in our former lives, we had never turned to violence. Money had lured us into the jungle as an answer to our hunger and desperation. The Commandant glorified our exploits and reshaped our vulnerable young minds. Vengeance drove me. Rage colored my blood.

I would avenge Dieng's death. I would make them pay for stealing one more person from me. Madness pumped through my heart. I was driven to kill. I fired wildly. I lost track of my bullets. I moved forward, into the open where I was pelted by dirt, branches, screeching birds, and bloodied lizards. Damn. They were launching grenades. The jungle shook. In the demon's hands, everything was uprooted.

Disoriented, I stumbled into the hole left by the grenade explosion.

I remembered the Commandant's instruction: "Boys, when the French throw them grenades, jump in the hole. A grenade never hits the same spot twice. You're safe there."

Searing pain shot through my right arm. Holding onto it with my left arm, I rolled onto my side. It stank in the hole. I heard the voices of boys and men yelling for help, gunshots, distorted bird cries and the sounds of crashing trees. Insects buzzed around fallen bodies. My pain intensified. The putrid smell made my stomach lurch. What caused it? I saw no blood. When I looked down, I smelled burning skin. My sleeve was charred, and so was my arm – what was left of it. The fuckin' asshole Commandant did not tell us the hole would be so damn hot. My arm was on fire.

I reached for a few leaves, stuffed them up the remnants of my sleeve. I clenched my teeth on a branch to muffle my howling. Then everything went black and silent.

***

I woke up on a cot among patched-up soldiers and boys dripping blood. I looked for Dieng among the disarray of broken flesh and pain. Then I remembered. I saw Dieng lying there, his legs blown off. There's nothing I could have done. He was going to die. I had to leave him there. The damn traitor was shooting at us. Tears ran down my face. I did not care. The mix of blood, smoke, dirt, and tears tasted salty and bitter. *Why did I come to this damn place?* I promised myself to kill as many enemies as possible for Dieng. The money did not matter anymore. I would not leave till I got every goddamn one of them.

***

I was back in the jungle the next day. The Commandant had to keep feeding the front line. He pushed us right back out there unless we were too damaged to hold a gun. No one needed to show me the way. Dieng's blood fueled my rage. I was determined to shoot every one of them, make them pay for robbing me of my friend. I wanted to cause pain. I was done losing.

Wrapped around a rubber-tree branch like a lizard, with my gun pressed against my chest, I waited for the signal announcing the enemy's presence. Sweat poured off my forehead.

"I am safe up here," I repeated to myself in an attempt to stay calm.

I shook my head violently to get rid of the sweat and cast off my doubts. My fingers curled around the bolt and the trigger while I steadied my other hand on the butt of the rifle. No longer a strange weapon, it felt right between my hands. It was mine and I controlled it. No part of me felt familiar. I would kill lots of these bastards and bring back some guns. The Commandant would praise me. I would make him ignore my bad arm. I would stay and fight until every single invader was dead. They would pay for killing my friends.

I heard the signal. "Woo-ta-woo."

I squinted, looking for the oddly shaped hats the traitors wore. Nothing.

"Wait, boy, wait. Be patient," I muttered to myself.

Cocking my head, I listened for the unnatural breathing of men holding guns, waiting for their death. At the first sight of gunmetal reflecting through the leaves, I aimed and pulled the trigger. It was a mere reflex.

"Aahh … merde." ("Aahh … shit.")

The sound of unrestrained weight hitting the ground rose above the jungle's voice. I leaped from the tree and shoved my knee into the fallen soldier's rib cage, raised my bayonet, and slaughtered him. I refused to look into his eyes. My mind turned off the volume on his shouts. Despair, anger and revenge coursed through my veins, empowering me to make this kill matter. How many more times would I seek vengeance before Dieng's death would be paid for?

"*Ka! Ka!*" I shrieked while stabbing the half-dead Frenchman again and again.

A crazed voice came from behind me. "*Gilles. Mais, où es-tu, merde, Gilles?*" ("Gilles. But where are you, shit, Gilles? ")

I could not make out the words, but recognized the desperation in the voice. It echoed my cry the day Dieng was killed.

I spun around. A few meters away, I saw a man with dark skin, taller and skinnier than me. Killing him would never quash what I felt on seeing my friend butchered. That did not stop me. We were enemies and we were brothers in this hell. I raised my gun but my fingers hesitated.

The sound of him shrieking "Gilles!" reverberated in my ears. I faltered. He raised his gun and fired at me. Once, twice, three times. My body crashed to the ground. Lying on my back, everything slowed. I heard shots fired above and all around me. My vision blurred. I could make out dark green thatch against a brilliant blue sky. Death with a view. The throbbing in my stomach was the only thing real to me.

THUMP, thump, THUMP, thump.

For a moment, I thought it would be fine to just lie there. What else was there to do but wait? I rocked gently side to side, whispering a childhood lullaby. In this hell, I refused to imagine the comfort of my mother's voice. Pain surged through me. My heartbeat was chaotic. My breathing grew shallow. Opening my mouth wider for air, the gurgling got louder. I gave up and took in the blueness of the sky until it disappeared.

***

When I rolled onto my side, the pain jerked me back to reality. Five months after the ambush, my life was an unrelenting nightmare. Not even the golden liquid helped me make it through the night without bloody corpses crashing through my dreams. The liquor did quell the constant pain. I had taken five bullets to the gut; the camp doctor had done his best. My belly button resembled the work of a drunken tattoo artist who had used a bayonet tip instead of a scalpel. The doctor had removed three of the five bullets.

"Boney, the last two are in too deep. You'll be OK. These two won't bother you too much. You'll live, no problem."

If a soldier from our side had not been following me, I would have been left to die in that rotten wasteland — a dead snake. Piak, two years younger than me, never made it back from the ambush. No one knew if he was killed or captured. I hoped he had died quickly.

***

The truce came two months later. France and Indochina made peace. What did that mean?

One of the village boys who arrived for training with me broke down crying.

"This means we go home," he said.

There was no enemy left to fight. The Commandant gave us his final, drunken speech. We were returning home to our families. We had made him proud, fought like men, he said. We were boy soldiers now. We should never again be afraid. We should remember the others who had fought hard but had fallen. I had lost everyone in my unit: Dom, Serree, Dieng, and Piak. They all died. Beside my mother, they were the only people I had ever cared for. They were my brothers. We survivors raised our fists and shouted the names of our fallen brothers. None of us would ever forget.

I had lost my mother before going to the jungle. Better that way. No mother could have welcomed the Lek who returned to Surin. Better to be a true orphan.

CHAPTER FIVE

EYES CLAMPED shut, I lied curled up like a shrimp in a thin, faded-blue sarong. Hugging my knees, I felt neither cold nor discomfort. This absence of distress surprised me, as pain had been my steady companion.

I forced my right eye open. Darkness. With both eyes opened, I saw small red and green lights blinking against a backdrop of shadows. No sky, burning candles, or flickering oil lamps. The smell was singular — clean and, therefore, unfamiliar. Where were the odors of rotting mangoes, overripe tomatoes, and dog urine? The sounds, too, were foreign—beeps from machines, human snores, and gasps. What had become of the laments of scrounging rats and moaning dogs?

I held myself tighter. Afraid to close my eyes completely and unable to identify my surroundings, I squinted. A table came into view. I saw a half-empty tin cup and a bowl. A folded cloth rested on the bowl's rim. At the sight of water, I acknowledged my extreme thirst. But I rolled away from it, scared to drink from a cup that belonged to someone else.

I tried to recall what had happened. Then, in a flash, it all came to me. I saw myself hanging by a noose. I ran my fingers over my moist skin. No burns, no cuts on my neck. My stomach cramped and I coughed. The pain helped me to remember more. I had attempted to take my life, and not for the first time. A few weeks ago, only two months after returning from the jungle, I had tried to hang myself — and failed. So, I had tried again, and ended up here, wherever this was. I had figured a vermin like me would die without much effort. I shook my head in disgust.

"You awake, boy?" a voice asked.

I froze, retreated further into myself, and held my breath.

"You awake, boy? You moved, for first time in days."

I kept quiet.

"You all right? I call nurse for you?"

"Nurse? Where am I?"

"Surin Hospital."

"Hos-pi-tal," I said.

"You very lucky boy to be alive. People here say you sick with rat poison. Poor boy. That stuff kill you. Made for rats. Even dumb people know that. You can eat dog's food but not rat's food."

"How long have I been here?"

"Three days. First day, you really sick. You stink up the place with your vomit. You sleep two full days. Me think you never wake up. Nobody came for you. Where you from?"

"Nowhere." I wanted go back there, I mumbled to myself. I turned my back to him.

He sighed, then inhaled and exhaled in the slow rhythm of sleep.

With a growing awareness of my second failure, more self-loathing crept in. I was too stupid to even kill myself. I wanted to avoid the pain of death, but the pain of living was worse. I was sick of scrapping with dogs over food and sleeping with them on the ground or in filthy holes. I sneered at the irony. They fell asleep without a care, spared the pangs of conscience. I tossed and turned, unable to forget the memories of the jungle. I could no longer take this surviving day-to-day. Tomorrow I would leave this place. I would jump in front of the first train I saw. My life had to end. "Sorry, Mommy."

I closed my eyes, comforted by the thought that next time I would succeed. I would do it. I saw myself splattered on the tracks. I was not worried about the pain as my death would be quick. I hoped I would be reborn a worm.

***

A bright light beamed into my eyes. Perhaps it searched for a trace of hope. I squeezed my eyes shut. "Leave me alone."

"*Waan Jai*, sweetheart," a female voice said. "The boy moves. See that? He's awake."

Near me, the male voice chimed in: "Yes, he speak to me last night. He upset. I think he no have family."

A hand rubbed the area between my ribs and waist. The pressure on the sheet was light, the touch caring. Enjoying the sensation, I stayed still. When the hand withdrew, I exhaled. Then it touched my right shoulder. I waited for it to push me out of bed. It shook me lightly. If I kept my eyes closed, maybe the hand would stay forever. I felt its warmth through the sheet. Silently, I invited it to stay, the way one welcomes glowing embers on a cold night.

"Boy. Boy, wake up," she whispered.

Wishing to delay the moment when she withdrew her hand, I opened one eye. A middle-aged woman was looking at me. Curious eyebrows framed her large, brown eyes. She wore a white cotton blouse and sun-drenched sarong over her stooped spine. Her calloused hands surprised me. Only a moment ago her touch had felt so gentle. Her thick, silky, black hair was pulled back in the tradition of mature Thai women.

What did she notice when she looked at me? Disheveled hair of an orphan who had no one to comb it for him. Scrawny rib cage and concave stomach which shouted hunger. Rough feet from going barefoot. Discolored skin from fights with dogs over garbage, insect bites from sleeping outside, and a gnarled right hand. Did she see an abandoned teenager whose errant soul needed guidance or a fragile boy afraid of his own shadow? Where was the animal that had performed unspeakable acts while fighting in the jungle only weeks ago?

"What's your name?" she asked.

"Lek."

The man in the bed next to me propped himself onto his bony elbows. His crooked brown teeth, haggard look, and cloudy eyes told me he was 50 or 60 years old. But he may have been younger and just worn down by hard living. Many in my country looked like him — joyless and weary.

"Lek?" he asked. "That's a nickname. Your real name is what?"

His talk tumbled out in the careless way we village people fumble with words. Words are borrowed tools when you have never attended school. How, then, could you ever hope to master them? I snapped.

"Lek be how my mommy call me. That's good enough."

I hated how everyone wanted to know about my family. If I had one, they would have been with me. Why did it matter where I came from? I was here now. My body stiffened. I tucked the exposed parts under the sarong. I wanted to disappear. I had no explanation for myself. I should have been dead.

"Lek. We call you Lek," the woman said.

The lightness of my name rolled off her tongue echoing the fluttering softness of a butterfly's wings. My name had not been spoken this way for so long. I had forgotten that it could sound sweet.

"Where is your family? They come for you soon?"

"I no have family," I told the woman.

"Where do you live?"

The question hung in the air.

The man broke the silence. "The boy not make a mistake. He ate rat poison." Defiance colored his words. "He—"

"Shush," the woman snapped, her face contorted in anger.

The man shrugged and flopped back onto the bed. He closed his eyes and drifted off.

How did he know what I had done? Who had told him? I wondered if I should leave before they threw me out. The indignity of my life burned in my gut.

"Lek, open your eyes, look at me," the woman said. "How old are you?"

"17. I think."

"Do you know how to read and write?"

I closed my eyes and grinded my teeth.

She waited.

"No."

I wanted the conversation to go on, but I wanted to talk about something else. I detected a fragrance. It was not my mother's jasmine, but some other blossom. She must have been a mother. She exuded tenderness instead of pity. She offered me a sweet and juicy *rambutan*, not a smelly, oozing *durian*. I could accept a *rambutan* without holding my nose.

"Do you know the village where you were born?"

I whispered to keep her close: "It's a long train ride from here to the countryside."

"You need to go back," she said.

"Me family is dead. There is nothing there for me. No reason to go. I don't want to remember. I want to forget, forget everything about my stupid life."

"You're so young. You can make better life."

I opened my eyes and glared at her, impolite, daring her to tell me how. Killing myself was the only way out of the misery, hunger, and hellish memories.

I raised my voice. "Impossible. You no understand."

She put her hand on my shoulder. "Shush. Listen to me, Lek."

Her words and touch calmed me down, but I would not meet her gaze. I wanted to stop her from peering into my soul, where my bloodied past lived.

"You see, Lek, you must go back. It's your only hope. The temple must accept any boy from village where they were born. Many boys like you, they poor. They go be novice and study to be a monk. The temple will teach you to read and write. You have place to sleep. They give you food every day. You learn the Buddha way. You learn to not suffer so much."

The woman's plea was so genuine that it cut through the shame imprisoning me.

"They won't take me. They no accept bad boys. I steal and lie and … and do other things to survive." I shook my head, certain that the monks would reject me. She did not understand where I had been and what I had done.

"They will not remember me in the village. My parents took me to village when I was baby. It was very far from where they born. They wanted more work, better life for us. My father die very soon, when I was four. My mother, she die after that, one year later. I was only 5 years old when I go away. No one there in village from my family. No one to say I was born in that village. Poor people, when we die, nothing left, no memory, only our ghost."

"Lek, you're too young to give up. You go, someone will remember. The villages, they very small."

She lifted my chin and looked into my eyes. This frightened me. I did not know if I should believe her. But I wanted to.

"Give me you hand." Her eyes narrowed. She leaned closer.

I braced myself for a slap. I deserved it. She must have been upset with me for disagreeing with her.

She took my left hand, balled in a tight fist. She pried open my fingers one by one, dropped a few coins in my palm, and closed her hand around mine.

"You go to you village and find the temple. You be good boy, good novice. You learn read and write. Someday you'll be a monk. You make merit for you dead parents. Make merit for me and me sick husband, too. We have no children. You go."

CHAPTER SIX

ON THIS September morning, the breeze was cool as it flowed through the open train windows. The sun illuminated the countryside unfurling before me. Water buffaloes labored in fields bloated with golden rice. Trees sagged under the weight of mangoes ripe for picking. Piles of green coconut husks, gutted of their meat, browned in the open fields. Women in straw hats squatted and wiped their brows. Half-naked children flitted about, grabbing at roosters before their playmates could beat them to the noisy fowl. Wrinkled ladies bent over their walking sticks stared at nothing in particular. By the roadside, noodle carts, fragrant with young basil and dried chilies, held strips of pork and vats of boiling broth. The steam melded with the sultry air. The carts awaited hungry peasants and landowners who would eat shoulder to shoulder on unsteady wooden stools. Fruit pickers carved up mangoes, pink dragon fruits, golden pineapples, and smelly *durians*, which they sprinkled with chilies or sugar for a few *baht*.

The train meandered lazily as we left Surin behind. I let out a deep breath. I was on the train, not under it. Equal parts of fear and excitement colored my interior landscape. Anxiety stirred within me. Why was I choosing to return to the village that had made me an orphan? No one awaited my homecoming. This village held endings, not beginnings.

***

"Stop for Hua Rat and Ban Sawai Jeek in 10 minutes."

The announcement startled me. As the train approached the stop, my 17-year-old eyes peered out the window at the sun-drenched scene. Villagers welcomed the passengers with shouts of joy. Their loved ones had returned from the big city. Expectation filled the air.

When I left Ban Sawai Jeek at the age of five, I had no one and nothing. It was not a conscious choice, of course. I was too young for that. I simply wandered away from the place where my parents had died. No one noticed I had disappeared. No one missed me; I was certain. Poverty bestows the blessing and the curse of invisibility. I became responsible for myself in a world no one had taught me to understand. I was unprepared.

I returned as a young man shackled by a past full of shame and indignities. It was not only a train stop; it was a crossroads. There, in my natal village, I would claim my right to a family of my own — or I would join my parents in death.

***

A few passengers disembarked. They distributed their city treasures bundled in tattered purple cloth among their relatives, and shuffled away. They knew where they were going; they were going home.

The train platform was nothing more than a clearing. I stood there until the commotion faded into chatter, then stillness. I inhaled the long forgotten village air. I hoped it remembered its native son. The *bugambilias* flaunted their radiant fuchsia flowers against a backdrop of greens, ferns, bamboos, and encroaching bushes. Like me, the bushes had grown. Unlike me, they had flourished. Next to the train tracks, I noticed a wooden sign with carved letters that I did not recall. Worst of all, I could not read it.

I wavered between running to my old house to reconnect with the joys of my early boyhood and avoiding it. My stomach knotted. I wondered if the abbot would be at the temple. Perhaps he had traveled to another temple.

The path to my village lay beyond the tracks. With no possessions to slow me down, I walked at a pace that would lead me, before dark, to the only place I had ever called home. I worried that no one would recognize me except, perhaps, the town's old herb healer who had treated my father and my mother. I did a quick calculation in my head and realized he was probably dead. A new dread overtook me and slowed my steps. Although hope had crept into the small of my back, I knew hope resembles a snake charmer – it hypnotizes you to the danger of your desires.

After an hour or so, everything dimmed in the fading light. I encountered no one. The shadows of the bamboo groves loomed large. Spotting a fallen tree, I stopped to rest and think. I thought it would be better to sleep there. I could arrive at the temple fresh in the morning. The abbot will be in a better mood after a good night's sleep and breakfast.

Afraid to be seen, I stepped deeper into the forest. Coming upon a small clearing, I spent a few minutes sweeping brush aside to make a bed. The noises comforted me: the familiar melody of cicadas, frogs, and the wind. Many times, I had slept under the stars on the outskirts of Surin, to avoid nightly combat with flea-infested street dogs. My sleep had been light as I was conscious of every threat on four legs. I had not allowed myself a deep and restful sleep. I preferred to avoid the nightmares that deep sleep camouflaged. With the thornier branches pushed aside, I lay down, hands under my head, knees tucked in. Within a few minutes, I was tossing and turning.

***

Bang! Bang! Kaboom! Rat-a-tat! Bang! Bang!

A racket exploded high above me. Noises whizzed by. The percussive bursts split my head with the force of a machete. I tried to cover my ears, but my hands were pinned against my hips. I was mummified in a hammock strung between trees. My legs were paralyzed. Strands of the hammock filled my mouth, leaving me voiceless. I saw flares, shadows of darkened faces, and bursts of light from reflected metal. The sky mirrored daylight. I feared a downpour of sparks and fire. Were those bullets and grenades? What the hell was going on? Where was I? And then it hit me: I was in a bloody war zone.

The hammock straps snapped, and freed, I tumbled into darkness. I braced myself against the impending crash. My body passed through an opening. Thump. I landed on a cold, hard surface. My back wedged against a wall. My knees jammed under my chin. I reached in front of me and touched another wall. I gasped. I heard nothing. Darkness — black as a panther — surrounded me. I was entombed in a bell-shaped concrete structure.

I found my voice: "Help. Please help me." The echo of my words bounced off the empty space.

Nothing. I strained to hear but only perceived faint intonations. Chanting. Monks were chanting. Had I died? Was this a crematorium? No one but monks could enter these buildings. In a flash I got it. I was trapped in a pyre and was about to be incinerated.

I attempted to stand up and failed. I felt the walls. No openings, no exits. No escape. If I did not get out immediately, I would be squashed. The walls would press against me, crushing my body, grinding my bones against each other.

"Help! Someone help me. I don't want to die."

The barking of dogs startled me. They must have been close. Could they smell me? Would the barking attract attention? Then everything went quiet. I opened my eyes. The sun's morning rays filtered through the branches. I blinked. I wondered where I was. Gasping, I looked around and saw a fallen tree. I was in the forest where I had fallen asleep the previous night. My body relaxed. My chest heaved. I was soaked in sweat. Another nightmare. Would they ever end?

***

When the first rooster crowed, I left my forest bed and walked in the direction of my village. The trees leaned in, creating a shaded pathway to the temple grounds. Soon the recognizable triangular-shaped rooftop, covered in red tiles and yellow paint, emerged behind trees bent with age. It looked the same, but more weathered than the day of my mother's funeral.

From somewhere on the grounds, I heard sweeping. Two mangy dogs lay in the cracked dirt. A man in a monk's orange robe, with skinny, bare legs and deformed big toes, approached me. He stood straight, shoulders held high. His skin sagged off his bony frame. Out of respect and fear, I dared not look at him. The monk stood still and said nothing. Digging my toes into the dirt, I shifted my weight. Unable to bear the silence any longer, I spoke.

"*Sawadee. Kap.* Are you the abbot?"

"Yes."

I raised my head and looked at a face from my childhood that had grown wiser and softer.

***

I was grateful that the big trees shaded me. Waiting on the bench, I swung my right foot back and forth. I created a groove, using my toe as a shovel. Be careful, I thought, the ghosts might think I wanted to trip them up. My hands folded and unfolded a crease in my worn-out trousers. My drab, white cotton shirt hung to my knees.

The sound of unsteady feet grew louder. Without thinking, I bowed, extending my hands flat against one another in the traditional *wei* gesture. My mother had taught me to greet elders with respect. Because this was the abbot, I dropped my head and raised my hands even higher. After a full month, this much I had learned. Tradition required that I use the formal title of *Luang Por*, or respected father, when I addressed the abbot.

A now familiar voice spoke. "Are you ready?"

I nodded. "Yes, *Luang Por*."

Following the instructions I received the previous day, I presented myself to the abbot. With an unsteady hand and a worn blade, he shaved my head. He tapped my head. Eyes closed, I raised my head. The abbot scraped the dull razor over my eyebrows. The falling strands tickled my nose. I made sure not to twitch. All my facial hair was gone. The abbot stepped back.

"*Luang Por*, may I receive the ten novice precepts?"

Tradition required him to reply to this request; the abbot had to bestow the precepts upon me. In order to be ordained a novice, an apprentice monk, I had to accept them.

And so he began.

"You undertake to observe the rules of training: to refrain from taking life, being unchaste, speaking falsely; taking distilled and fermented intoxicants or drugs; taking food at the wrong time; dancing, singing, playing music, and seeing shows; using flowers, perfumes, and cosmetics for beautifying and adorning the body; using high and luxurious sleeping places and seats; accepting gold and silver."

I repeated word for word, without hesitation or mistakes.

"I hold my beliefs in the Buddha, the *Dharma*, and the *Sangha*," I said.

The abbot leaned over and handed me the orange novice garments: a *sabong* (under robe tied around the waist with a rope); an *ungsa* (to cover the chest); and a *jivorn* (the outer robe).

"*Nehn* Amporn, take your robe. Tomorrow you will join me and the four other novices for morning chants."

With that pronouncement, I acquired new clothes and a new name. *Nehn* would be the proper way to address me from then on. My mother had named me Amporn but I did not remember anyone ever having used it. I much preferred my real name to "hobo boy" which is what the market vendors in Surin called me. And that had been on a good day, when they were not angry and calling me "dirty scoundrel."

I repeated my new name to myself, *Nehn Amporn*. I liked it.

CHAPTER SEVEN

WE FILED out of the temple grounds in the morning darkness for my first round of collecting alms. I saw my old village for the first time since my return. The four novices trailed behind the abbot in order of seniority. I was the last in line.

No one would recognize me after so many years, my head shaven and my body covered by a robe. Unease filled my gut. I had morphed from vagrant to young man. I no longer stole or begged for food. That morning I was *Nehn* Amporn, a novice monk, accompanying the abbot in my hometown. My posture improved. I held my head a little higher, breathing in the village air. My heart skipped to the abbot's footfalls. I listened to the chants I would soon be able to chorus.

The excitement wore off as my alms bowl grew heavier. From the rear, away from the abbot, I glanced up without fear. I yearned for the familiarity of my hometown. Distant villages like this one, they grew, but they did not change much. The place lingered in your bones, and the minute you returned you expected to feel right at home. It held the magic of your childhood and the first experiences of growing up. But I did not belong to Ban Sawai Jeek, any more than it did to me. We shared no such bond.

Bored with the monotony of the ritual, my mind replayed the sudden turn my journey had taken in the last month. Small acts of kindness, initiated by a woman in the Surin hospital, had altered the course of my life. Before I asked to be accepted into the temple, the head villager, Swaki Pu Yai, told the abbot that he remembered a young boy who had been orphaned many years ago and had disappeared. He agreed with the abbot that if I claimed to be this young man, he saw no reason not to acknowledge me as a native son.

He also said that my forehead reminded him of my father, and my eyes were like my mother's. At first, these words reverberated in my soul. Maybe he could tell me more about my parents. But my fear of disappointment proved to be greater than my desire to hear something about my family that might be at odds with the memories I clung to in my darkest moments. And so, I refrained from approaching him. It also troubled me that if he did not remember my family, I would be indebted to him. Either outcome would be too much to bear. I shook my head to dispel these thoughts. Forget about it, I told myself. You are here now, a novice. That's all that mattered. Not how I got there.

Life at the temple had a rhythm. Each day I received food. I had a place to sleep and a monk who taught me. For the first time, my mind filled with new knowledge instead of plans of how to steal food. In the evenings I concentrated on remembering my lessons instead of trying to forget my past.

I had already memorized the basic chants, and much to the abbot's surprise, I recited many verses in ancient *Pali*. The language came to me without much effort. I listened, and then repeated the sounds in my head. With their odd harmony, they stuck in my mind. I could not forget them. *Nehn* Jirasak appeared unable to remember any of them, and *Nehn* Tep did not care at all. He could have been ordained much sooner but he did not want to be bound by the stricter novice precepts. He hated rules. So he waited until the last moment, only a few days ahead of me. He had been here almost six months before his head and eyebrows were shaved. He boasted that his family would come for him the moment his father's health recovered. Unlike the rest of us poor boys, he would be a farmer, not a monk. He often disregarded the rules and blamed others. I had suffered the wrongs of his type before. I could teach him a few tricks. I felt certain that our paths would not stay joined for long.

Nehn Tep tugged at my robe. He did so in a sneaky way, as to avoid the abbot's noticing.

"Stop," I mumbled under my breath.

His smile lacked innocence. The abbot looked down at me with displeasure.

Stupid boy, I reprimanded myself. *Pay attention. You must please the abbot. This is not a game. Your father will not come for you.* Lost in thought, I had fallen behind the others after the abbot blessed the last villagers. *Nehn* Tep was just trying to even the score. He hated that I learned *Pali* faster than he did. He intimidated the other boys with his rough edges. I ignored him. I had survived the jungle; he could not bully me.

Back at the temple, I swept the yard with grand strokes. I wanted to attend to my assigned task right away so the abbot would know my virtues. Within a few moments, dust flew everywhere, and the roosters ran for cover. Even the dogs sprawling in the dirt moved to avoid the tornado I created.

"*Ne-hn* Am-porn," the Respected Father whispered, emphasizing each syllable.

I deciphered the sounds rather than heard my name.

The other monks looked on.

"Novices must not call attention to themselves. You should be mindful of your every movement. Embody calmness."

I froze, held my breath, and lowered my head, waiting for some form of physical reprimand. None followed. Although thrashing temple boys was common, our abbot believed the practice to be inappropriate for novices. I offered a deep *wei*.

"Yes, *Luang Por*."

To slow down my sweeping, I disciplined myself to recite a full verse of chant between strokes. How different life could be from one place to another.

Out of the corner of my eye, I saw *Nehn* Tep sprawling in the shade of a fig tree. I did not think sitting under the *bodhi* tree would enlighten him as it did the Buddha. His downcast head did not hide his arrogant attitude. With a gaze in his direction, I mumbled to myself, "We are not done, you and I."

CHAPTER EIGHT

YOU MIGHT say I was like a peacock with its tail tucked in. I did not wish to court disaster with the abbot, but I wanted to shed my plain saffron cloth and fan out my plumage for all to see. Since my return to my village three months earlier, I had been doing something magical — learning to decode the swirls and strokes that come together to form words. I could read! I devoured everything I saw on the page, even those words I did not yet understand. I no longer felt apart from the world. The more I learned, the more tail feathers I seemed to acquire.

The Buddha's teachings were founded on two principles: the Four Noble Truths and the Noble Eightfold Path. The Truths, as I understood them, intrigued me. What troubled me was the Path, the practice that would lead me away from suffering. The Noble Eightfold Path allowed neither pride nor attachment. My desire to learn filled me with both. My curiosity, flamed by my eagerness, drove my unquenchable thirst for knowledge. I was determined to grasp the meaning of every word. I read everything aloud. Words were sweeter to me than mango sticky rice. The pleasant flavor of syllables flew from my eyes and onto my tongue. I felt confident that in just a few more months, I would master the ability to write. The thought that I would be able to accomplish this filled me with pride.

The abbot entered and sat at the front of the *sala*, an open pavilion, with his back to the statue of the meditating Buddha. Gold leaves of adornment peeled away from the Buddha, like skin from a fruit or petals from a flower. The abbot sat cross-legged in the common *mudra* position known as 'Calling the Earth to Witness.' His left hand rested in his lap, palm up; his right arm extended in front of him, fingers pointing to the ground. This position embodies the moment that the Buddha reached enlightenment under the *bodhi* tree. I recognized its meaning, and I aspired to live it. Before the Buddha reached enlightenment, I wondered if he had misbehaved.

I bowed and cast my gaze toward the gleaming floor polished by thousands of bare feet over the years. I had to keep my head lower than those of the senior monks. About midpoint in the chanting, the older monks sank into themselves while they meditated or drifted off. I needed to keep an eye on their position to make sure I kept my head below theirs.

'*Araham sammashambuddho Bhagava.*' (The Noble One, the Fully Enlightened One, the Exalted One.) The abbot recited in a low monotone with slight changes in pitch from time to time. The tone evoked the stirring of thick coconut milk.

We novices responded: *'Buddham Bhagavantam abbhidavemi.'* (I bow low before the Exalted Buddha.)

I recited the *Pali* verses with the ease of childhood lullabies. My mind drifted to a corner of the room where my thoughts were free to wander. Why did *Phra* Teacher become a monk? With his intelligence he could teach at a large school, maybe even in Bangkok. Yet he sat there, day after day, teaching silly boys like me who would simply return to the paddy fields. And the abbot? He exemplified the qualities of goodness and a warm heart. Why did he not take a wife and have children? He could read and write; he could find work with good pay. He would be a kind father. Why do these men stay here? Why do they not yearn to leave, the way we novices do?

A big toe stabbed my back. It must be *Nehn* Tep, the little monkey. Would he ever stop bothering me? He lived to distract me, make me falter, and disgrace myself. He was more of a stupid boy than I. At night, when I tried to read whatever books I could find, *Nehn* Tep smothered the flame of the coconut oil lamp to annoy me. He had no interest in reading. He wanted to farm his family's land someday. He needed to learn how to interpret the clouds and the winds, he said, not letters on the pages. *What a fool.*

My face reddened. I dropped my head lower, grateful that neither the abbot nor *Phra* Teacher had caught my nasty thoughts.

When the *suat*, chanting, had ended and the Respected Father had gone, I quickly left to avoid meeting *Nehn* Tep. His taunting unnerved me. My internal resolve weakened. My serenity was troubled. I envied his impending return home to his parents and siblings. I wandered the temple grounds wrestling with my frustrations and the Buddha's instruction on inner peace.

"*Nehn* Amporn, you are resting from your studies this evening?" said *Phra* Teacher, dragging me back to the present.

"Come sit with me."

I had never been to *Phra* Teacher's *kutti*, his small private space where he slept and studied. It consisted of four bamboo stakes, two noisy steps, and a narrow ledge for sitting which ran along a large opening leading into the only room. From where I stood, I could see it had mosquito-netting hanging from the ceiling, an oil lamp, and a pile of saffron cloth. In the corner, books were piled on the floor, next to a straw mattress. Only the senior monks had a *kutti*.

Slowly I approached him, unsure of where and how to sit. His left arm appeared from under his dark robe and gestured to the space next to him on the ledge. For the first time, I noticed his upper arm was tattooed with some *Hah Taew*, the Five Sacred Lines, but I could not tell which ones. His robe fell back into place before I could decipher the words. I turned to face him, as a student to his teacher, but looked down to show respect.

He nodded and gently turned away from me to gaze out onto the temple grounds.

I appreciated this small kindness. It would be easier to avoid looking into his eyes.

Phra Teacher initiated the conversation. "*Nehn* Amporn, what troubles you?"

"Nothing, *Phra* Teacher. Just trying to memorize today's *Dhammapada* verse. 'There is happiness in life, happiness in friendship, happiness in family, happiness in a healthy body and mind, but when one loses them …'"

"'One suffers.'" His words trailed off into the night.

"*Nehn* Amporn, talk with me. I am an old man. Tonight my bones ail me and I cannot find sleep. Tell me, what afflicts you?"

I remained silent — and bewildered. I expected him to give me teachings while I listened. He surprised me with his question. *Phra* Teacher had told us he was born before 1900 when our country was still called Siam. This was the first time I had heard that a country had changed its name. I thought only people could do so.

Phra Teacher studied under Buddhist masters in the oral tradition, without books. In his childhood, boys took charge of the water buffaloes at the age of six. They feared ghosts and wore magical amulets left behind by travelling forest monks.

"*Nehn* Amporn, you are a very promising student of the Buddha's instructions. Do you wish to be ordained a monk?"

I chose to ignore the question.

"Why did you become a monk, *Phra* Teacher?"

"I'll tell you my story, but you must keep it to yourself, *Nehn* Amporn."

Phra Teacher was a happy Buddha look-alike. His robe swelled from a rounded belly and exposed his fleshy right shoulder. His plump face made him appear ageless. His pudgy hands were soft from lemongrass oil. A patch of wispy, black hair balanced on his head. His eyes sparkled and transmitted serenity. His bulbous nose overpowered his face.

"*Kap*, Yes," I said, leaning toward him.

"I come from near the country of Laos, up north from the province of Nan. Up there, people speak *Kammuang*. I have not seen my home for a very long time. All my relatives, they are gone. I have outlived them. My family was very big. My father thought all his children could help with the small land he rented. When my eldest brother reached the age of 11, he was responsible for caring for us so my parents could work the fields together. You see, in those days you did not think about being rich. If you had vegetables to eat, rice to harvest, and fresh water to drink, then everyone was happy."

Old monks speak the way blind people walk … slowly, often taking the longer path. I wanted to understand why *Phra* Teacher stayed at the temple. Still, I kept silent and listened. I focused on his mouth with its full lips.

"My village was a small, isolated one. We had a river for catching fish and swimming. I was captivated by the fish fights. These small animals can kiss each other for hours until one decides to fight. Then there is a frenzy. They bite through each other's scales, sometimes ripping off a fin. I used to love to feed them mosquitoes. It was a good distraction from my responsibilities."

I had difficulty imagining *Phra* Teacher as a little boy. He appeared too wise. I wanted him to tell me how he lost his fear of ghosts and how he dealt with thoughts about his family. I let him talk.

"I followed in my brothers' footsteps. I studied only for a few months and then helped with whatever I could. I was happy to be in charge of the family buffalo once I was old enough to have my own responsibilities. My other brothers tended to the rice, which was backbreaking work. One of my sisters had to look after the ginger. You see, I knew the only path was the same one my father took. I knew studying was useless. My village was my whole world."

I thought of Tep and wondered if *Phra* Teacher was unruly too. I could not stay silent any longer.

"What happened? Why did you give up, *Phra* Teacher, and become a monk?"

My stomach tightened. I feared that my disrespect would put an end to our conversation. *Phra* Teacher seemed undisturbed, however. Instead, he folded his arms over his belly. His gaze moved farther into the distance.

"My parents were simple people. They feared ghosts. We spent a lot of time making sure to the spirits were kept happy so we would not suffer a bad harvest. But even with all the offerings of rice, sweets, and daily morning prayers at the family shrine, grasshoppers infected the harvest. Nothing grew."

"But your parents did not do anything bad to make this happen?"

"No, *Nehn* Amporn, they did not. Still, we were hungry all the time. Sometimes we ate worms or dirt to put something in our stomach. We were always sick. We had no choice. The only solution was for one of us boys to go and live at the temple. To make merit ... and, well, it was one less mouth to feed."

He grew quiet. I was afraid he would fall asleep.

"Why you, *Phra* Teacher?".

"I was at the right age, two or three years away from the time boys become ordained."

"Your father forced you?"

"No. My father said if I did not want to become a monk after one or two years, he would send my next younger brother. That made me feel better."

The distance between *Phra* Teacher and me dissolved. For a moment he set aside his chosen role as a monk to speak to me as I imagined a father would to a son. He wanted me to understand something about life, while I overflowed with questions. I wanted answers that led to a different path than his. I wanted a family.

"Why did you stay, *Phra* Teacher? Did you not want your own family?"

"At first, learning *Pali* was very difficult. Then I had to study all that I had missed—basic mathematics, grammar, and history. My father was not informed that I would mostly be studying the Buddha's ancient language. I think my father secretly hoped they would teach me to read and write Thai. Then I could get a job in a bigger city to support the family."

"What happened?" I asked.

"Once I began to study, I found it was easy for me. I got my first certificate, the same one you received already, for primary course. The abbot told me I should continue to study. He said if I worked hard, I could finish all nine grade levels of *Pali* and be named *Maha*. You know what *Maha* means, *Nehn* Amporn, don't you?"

He paused and sipped water from a bamboo cup.

"Yes, it means 'great,'" I said. The moonless night obscured my smile. He continued.

"Then, I had it in my head that I could earn the title of *Maha*."

So *Phra* Teacher was a peacock, too.

Phra Teacher lowered his head.

"Did you become a *Maha*, *Phra* Teacher?"

"Yes."

"Was your father proud? Did he want you to come home to your village then?"

"The family situation had improved a little; there was a better harvest that year. My father said it was because I was making merit for the family. He was convinced that if I dedicated my life to studying the Buddha's word and carrying out all the rituals for the villagers, such as the wedding ceremonies and funerals, bad luck would go away and never return."

"So you had to stay a monk."

My heart ached with disappointment for him.

"*Nehn* Amporn, I already knew that I would not be returning home. The temple had become my family."

He glanced at me. My eyes fixed on the hem of my robe. Beneath the fabric, I dug my nails into my thighs.

I could not lie to *Phra* Teacher. I could not promise to stay.

"*Nehn* Amporn, you are a very good student. I think you have already seen much of life outside this small village. Maybe you need to go to a larger temple after the rainy season. The Buddha, he traveled much before he sat under the *bodhi* tree. Before the *Sangha* Reforms were initiated in 1902, when I was barely six, monks traveled all over Siam — I mean Thailand — to teach *Dharma*."

His words lingered on the edges of my soul. One question remained on my lips, however.

"*Nehn* Amporn, *Phra* Teacher is an old man. We have talked a long time. We will have to finish some other day."

"One more question, *Phra* Teacher, please," I blurted out as I noticed his eyes drooping. I needed to ask him this one question as there might never be another chance.

"*Phra* Teacher, you did something good. You became a monk and your family's fortunes were better. But what if you did something very bad in your life, before you were a monk, before you were a novice, or before you even knew about the Buddha's teachings?"

My heart pounded. *Phra* Teacher remained as still as an egret.

"I wonder ... if you become a good monk after you made a few big mistakes, will you still be reincarnated into a lower life-form?"

Phra Teacher's eyes were on me again. I looked away.

"*Nehn* Amporn, were you in trouble before you came to our temple?"

I swallowed hard. I wanted to honor my vows and I did not want to lie to him.

"My parents died when I was 5 years old. I was alone until I came to this temple. Sometimes I had to do very bad things to get food."

My shoulders stiffened and my jaw locked. I hoped I had not spoken a lie by using such vague language. I braced myself for the answer.

Phra Teacher stayed silent a long time. Then he placed his hand on my bare shoulder. His warm touch surprised me. His tenderness traveled to a place inside me, which had been hollowed out years ago.

"*Nehn* Amporn, I do not know the mysteries of reincarnation, but if you follow the Middle Way, you do not need to worry about your next life. Remember, *Tham Dee, Dai Dee, Tham Chua, Dai Chua* (Good actions bring good results; bad actions bring bad results). Good night, *Nehn* Amporn." With those words, he struggled to his feet and walked away into his *kutti*.

Once I was alone, the darkness of the night, which moments ago had made possible our intimate talk, left me feeling desolate.

Without any guiding light, I tiptoed toward the cottage where I slept with the other novices. From behind, a sudden sharp jab in the ribs stopped me. Without turning around, I swept my right arm back to grab whatever or whoever had attacked me. With all my weight, I threw the attacker to the ground and pressed my right knee into his lower spine. My left hand reached for the attacker's hair. But it was a shaved head. Immediately I went for his mouth and smothered it with my hand. I needed to muzzle him. I scratched in the dirt for a stone to cut his flesh.

"Who are you? What do you want from me?" I said.

"Nothing, *Nehn* Am—"

Tep's voice cut through me. His whimpering lessened my rage. My body froze. My hands stiffened around his bare arm.

"If you say anything to anyone, anyone at all about this, I promise I will come to you in the still of the night and finish you off. You hear me?"

Nothing.

I dug my knee deeper into his back. "Answer me," I spat.

"I promise, *Nehn* Amporn. I'll never tell."

I released my grip, struggled to my feet, and ran toward the temple gate. I felt the memories of the jungle closing in on me.

CHAPTER NINE

THREE YEARS had passed since I had stood at the edge of my life at Surin hospital. I was only 17 when I returned to my hometown of Ban Sawai Jeek. Unsure of myself, but deeply hungry for a family, I never imagined then that I would study at the *wat*s of Ayutthaya, Angtong, and eventually Bangkok.

It was five in the morning when I arrived on the banks of the Chao Phraya River just outside our capital city. The swarms of nighttime mosquitoes were just retreating. A faint light stretched from the horizon to Tha Tien Pier as our ferry approached the shore. I sensed the waking city before I saw it. Confused waves lapped against the banana-shaped boats in the midst of purposeful water traffic. On the barges, buffaloes appeared in silhouette against the lightening sky. Figures hunched over homemade crafts and mountains of mangoes. Herds of people crammed the ferries in transit or crowded the piers. Sounds from humans, animals, and machinery combined in a discordant melody punctuated by the intermittent clanking of metal against metal. The stench from fishing boats made me pinch my nose until the sting of petrol burned my throat. My stomach pulsated with the commotion.

I had arrived in Bangkok. I had left what we Thais call the up-country, the rural area in the north. The old people in the countryside called our capital city Thailand. It did not make sense to me. Perhaps this allowed them to preserve their love for the past. They could still refer to the country as their beloved Siam as if the new modern capital city was a different place they did not belong to.

I preferred the full ceremonial name of Bangkok that I learned as a novice. Composed from both *Pali* and *Sanskrit*, very few of us remembered it: *Krung Thep Amon Rattanakosin Mahinthara Ayuthaya Mahadilok Phop Noppharat Ratchathani Burirom Udomratchaniwet Mahasathan Amon Piman Awatan Sathit Sakkathattiya Witsanukam Prasit.* The city of angels, the great city, the residence of the Emerald Buddha, the impregnable city of Ayutthaya of God Indra, the grand capital of the world endowed with nine precious gems, the happy city, abounding in an enormous Royal Palace that resembles the heavenly abode where the reincarnated God reigns, a city given by Indra and built by Vishnukarn.

I thought about the magic found in Bangkok's name and implored it to accompany me while I found my path in that gigantic city.

My legs ached from sitting during the 12-hour boat ride through the *klongs* (canals). I stepped onto the pier, clutching my only worldly possession: a satchel the color of dried-up marigolds. It held two books of chant, one dictionary, and my sarong. The rough weave of the bag identified me as a village boy.

The buses were not yet operating. The taste of curry from the day before lingered in my mouth. With the thought of food, my stomach contracted. People loaded and unloaded their wares on the wharf with such monotony. They were oblivious to the excitement that surged within me.

Four monks stepped onto the pier. I took this as a good omen. I *wei*-ed to the wrinkles of experience creasing their pale faces. They nodded back to acknowledge me as a young novice. I asked for the directions to *Wat Tuek*. A soft voice, the same as all the others I had heard in the temples, directed me to a place near the China market. The familiarity of the monk's tone surprised me. For some reason, I had expected city monks to sound different.

The first morning bus, overloaded with passengers, grumbled to a stop a few feet away. It had the same tired red-and-white markings of public transportation found in the villages. In deference to my robe, someone motioned for me to climb aboard. Even as a novice, I traveled without paying. I avoided the bus driver's eyes. I did not know the ways of Bangkok. He *wei*-ed in my direction, shrugged his shoulders, and shifted into gear. Once seated on the bench reserved for monks, I heaved a sigh. I did not realize I had been holding my breath.

It was 1957, the year that marked a transformative time for my country. The government had begun to exploit our natural resources. The elder monks complained that while the government promoted Thailand as the latest tiger of Asia, it implemented policies such as the National Development Programs that killed spiritual beliefs. Everything became commoditized. Farmers and fishermen no longer produced solely for their families and villages, but shipped our goods to faraway places well beyond our borders. Foreigners with different beliefs converted our young people to unknown Gods. Traditional dress was lost to shirts and pants. The village *wat*s were emptying and the cities were bulging.

Since this was my first experience outside the villages, I had no point of comparison. Everything appeared modernized. No matter where I looked, this oversized city offered visual distractions. Ahead, I noticed a strange bus. Hooked to wires, it traveled on railroad tracks in the middle of the widest road I had ever seen. The metallic beast emitted an ear-splitting squeal when it stopped. I covered my ears. People: one, two, five, 10, 15 or more disembarked. Motorized bicycles, tricycles, and pushcarts competed for space on the roads. They reminded me of flying ants swarming in great numbers, yet they never collided.

When I reached the temple a half-hour later, I was still within the city's borders. The monks in Bangkok lived very differently to their counterparts in the rural areas. They were stuffed four to a room barely large enough to hold two adults. Someone told me some even paid the abbots to secure their stay. This confused me. The *Sangha* rules prohibit monks from handling money except for receiving offerings either from the families of the deceased, or newlyweds, so they can make merit. This was how the abbot explained it to us in the village. Offerings were turned over to the temples for their maintenance. I wondered if monks in Bangkok had jobs outside the temples.

Without money or connections, I knew this temple would not accept me. I returned to the pier. From there, I would find a way. I would have to start at the beginning, again.

For the second time that day, I rode a bus away from the pier. Curious as to where it would take me, I chose bus number 12 randomly. After traveling until only a few passengers were left, the bus stopped at the end of a rice field. The last two villagers, struggling under the weight of their unruly loads wrapped in fabric shreds, left. The bus driver turned to me, *wei*-ed, and pointed to the door. I brushed past him on my way out. He nodded, without bothering to bring his hands together in a formal *wei*. He must have grown tired of monks who rode his bus for free.

The outskirts of the city appeared empty. Lime and dark green grooves scarred the rural land and seemed to go on forever. Following into the distance the rows before me, I noticed a cross on an odd-looking house. It drew me. I wondered if I walked in that direction whether I would find a small temple that would take me in.

The cross grew closer. I picked up my stride, and kicked the odd stone on the clay path. I heard the abbot's voice in my mind.

"*Nehn* Am-porn. This is time for contemplation. Novices must walk slowly and be mindful."

I waved his voice away like an ox using his tail to swat a persistent fly.

I was tired and thirsty. My robe clung to me in the increasing humidity. The building would give me much-needed relief from the strong sun. A small tower with a cross sat on a square shaped house. A crooked sign with unfamiliar letters hung from the house. *Damn*.

I lowered my head the moment the word escaped. Some habits were hard to lose. Even after three years of temple life, my instincts from the old days still snuck up on me.

I shrugged my shoulders and readjusted my satchel. Whatever this place was, it mystified me with its foreign language and curious architecture. Again, I felt the empty space in my stomach, which could have been loneliness or hunger, or both. The lunch from the day before had been a long time ago, so it must have been hunger. I moved on.

The few huts along the path reminded me of my village. They suffered from the same neglect, except these homes were surrounded by some scavenged possessions: reclaimed pieces of wood, aged baskets, and rusted harvesting tools. Here, too, the dogs appeared sickly and uncared for, with exposed wounds. Snouts to the ground, they glanced up. They judged me unworthy of their sniffing. I never looked at abandoned dogs for too long.

After a while, I spotted a worn, yellow flag on a bamboo pole, announcing a temple ahead.

The sight of this emblem reminded me of the first time I had asked *Phra* Teacher about these flags.

"Why do the temple flags depict an old wagon wheel like the ones on oxen carts?"

In his sage voice, he had answered, "*Nehn* Amporn, you must learn this. The 12-spoke wheel, what we call the *Wheel of Dharma*, forms an important part of the Buddha's teachings."

The expression on my face must have shown my confusion.

"It represents the concept of conditionality that the Buddha teaches. It is the natural law of interdependence. It is irrelevant whether one is enlightened or not. It guides everybody's life. Remember the *Pali* canon you memorized: 'When there is this, there is that. With the arising of this, that arises. When this is not, neither is that. With the cessation of this, that ceases.'"

I had nodded.

Then *Phra* Teacher had left me to reflect on the verses. This memory immediately taunted me. My mind twisted the words around into disorder: "When there are bad past actions, there is bad future. With the arising of wanting, bad luck arises. When there is no family, neither will there be. With the cessation of life within the robes, forward progress ceases."

I hated how my mind and soul battled over my future like *muay* Thai fighters. I always wondered how much longer I could keep my heart safe from the assaults launched by my mind. Reason sabotaged my hopes and dreams. Would those mental onslaughts ever end?

The flags led me to the *Wat Huay Kwang*, home to only three monks. The abbot, *Luang Phu* (Great Grandfather) said I could stay. Because the monks were at least 30 years older than me, perhaps this abbot hoped more young monks would come. I wished only for a place that would allow me to study without making too many demands.

After being assigned a corner of the shared cottage, I joined my new *Luang Ta* (Great Uncles). I addressed them in this respectful manner to acknowledge their age and to gain their favor. These monks were from the meditative tradition. They had taken vows of silence. I expected to learn little from them. I should have considered myself fortunate. They would be more accepting of my long hours of study. I noticed the abbot skipped a few verses during the chants. The Great Uncles seemed accustomed to this. They skipped them too. Perhaps this *wat* would bring me good fortune by providing me a quiet place to learn faster.

After a few days, the quietness of the *wat* oppressed me. The silence provided a place in which my conflicting desires wandered. In one year I would be 21 years old. I would have to decide whether to ordain as a monk. I needed to complete my studies. I still required my high school equivalency. If I left the robes, I would have to go to a State school. I had no money to pay for books, food, or a place to live. The answer was clear: I had to stay in the robes. It was the only logical solution. Yet my desire for another life grew every day. Among the 227 vows of ordination, one required me to remain celibate. I reminded myself that my yearnings, like those of fighting roosters, could not be confined to a cage forever. There would come a time when this rooster would have to fight or fly away.

CHAPTER TEN

Ayutthaya, Thailand, 1958

ON MARCH 11, three days before the full moon, I turned 21. Seeing no other choice, I informed the abbot that I wished to ordain. The abbot decided that the ceremony should take place before the rainy season. He chose June 10, the day of the full moon, as the auspicious date. The stone had been cast.

After a mere 12 hours of fasting in preparation for taking my vows, my stomach cramped and cried out for food. My body suffered. In the temple I had grown unaccustomed to the hunger pangs of my childhood. I was like a squawking fledgling. My books lay scattered about me. Although the seasonal heat had already peaked, I lay around in my *sabong*. The other monks with whom I shared the *kutti* were avoiding me until after my ordination. I had not turned a page in hours. What a waste of time. My mind played tricks on me, wandering in and out of present awareness.

In my dreams, I saw myself rolled up like a piece of pork in banana leaves — the same way I would have to wear the new saffron robe paid for by my sponsoring family chosen by the abbot. In these dreams, the fabric was so confining that I could barely breathe. Ink poured from my body — evidence of all the books I had read. My dismembered hands, stained in blood, lay on the ground. On waking, I would shake my head so violently, I was surprised when it did not fall off.

The thought of wearing the robe gnawed at me. I had decided to take my vows to calm my internal torment. The problem was that my head and my heart refused to make peace with each other. I needed to calm the storm raging within, which pitched my past and my future against each other.

***

I stood before 10 very old monks at *Wat Ban Bang* Temple in Ayutthaya, about 50 miles north of Bangkok. The Burmese had destroyed the city in the 18th century, leaving only the *prang*, the towers, and large monasteries. The monks were here to witness my ordination. I had to answer all the questions posed by the abbot.

"My name is *Nehn* Amporn. I have been trained by *Phra* Pan."

"Do you have leprosy, *Naga* Amporn?" the abbot asked.

"No," I answered.

It pained me to look at these men. They appeared shadows of their former selves. Unlike *Phra* Teacher, who resembled a happy Buddha, they could have been mistaken for forest mendicants. Their robes and skin were faded and frayed. Yet, the wisdom in their eyes compelled me to join them in the *Sangha* – the brotherhood of monks.

The possibility of enlightenment should always be the only true motivation for joining the monastic life. But as I stood there, I knew my goal was different. I was seeking intellectual enlightenment. I wished to become educated and respectable. Sensing that I was nearing a precipice, I stopped myself from thinking further. I needed to banish these thoughts from my heart, or risk tumbling into the abyss. The choice of becoming a monk, of completing the ordination, was mine and mine alone. No father or mother had requested that I do it for the benefit of our family.

"Have you received your parents' permission to be ordained?"

"Yes."

I knew that in choosing to take my vows, I had found the only way to escape an intolerable life, something I could not accomplish with two failed suicide attempts. I had to pay for my past mistakes and ignorance. Then, perhaps, if I became a good monk, I would be born into the next life luckier and smarter. The Buddha's verses flashed through my mind: "He was not a monk just because he lives on the alms of others. Not by adopting outward form does one become a true monk ..."

In that moment, my heart had to accept what my mind already knew: that I would never have a family. Accepting this truth was the only way that I could become a true monk.

"Are you a human being?" the abbot asked.

"Yes."

"Are you a man, *Naga* Amporn?"

Phra Teacher had instructed me about the Buddhist legend that told of a clever snake, a *naga*, which turned itself into a human being to become ordained as a monk. The monastic rules emanated from ancient times; they had remained the same since the Buddha's time. If an ordination was carried out mistakenly, it was still valid. The story went on to say, the *naga* fell asleep in the *kutti* it shared with other monks. During the night, it was transformed into its original form. One of the monks awoke and was frightened to find a powerful serpent sleeping next to him. The Buddha found out about those events. He summoned the *naga* and asked it to leave the *Sangha*.

The snake began to cry, for it did not want to leave the order. The Buddha shared the Five Precepts for human beings and encouraged the snake to be true to them so it could be reincarnated as a human being in its next life. Once this was achieved, the *naga* could ordain as a novice and eventually as a monk. The Buddha felt such compassion for the animal's sorrow, he decided that, on the day novices ordain, they would be called "*Naga*" from the moment they first entered the temple until they took their final vows.

"Are you a man, *Naga* Amporn?" The abbot repeated the question, scrunching his hairless eyebrows at my failure to maintain the rhythm of the questions and answers.

With great effort, I pushed the sound out of my mouth.

"Yes."

I was determined to charm the snake within me into eternal sleep. I was seeking out enlightenment. I detached from my desire for family and knowledge. Perhaps Mother awaited me there, in that next life.

"Are you fully 20 years old?" asked the abbot.

"Yes, I am 21 years old."

"Are your bowl and robes complete?"

"Yes."

Phra Maha Panya, the senior and most emaciated monk in attendance, proposed three times, in accordance with the rules, that I be admitted to the *Sangha*. All ten, silent monks chanted their final approval. My tension eased in the way rice spills from a broken basket.

"From this moment, you shall be known as *Bikkhu* Visalo," the abbot announced. I was a monk.

CHAPTER ELEVEN

MISS GLOVER stood at the front of the class. Dressed in a dark blue suit, her skirt covered her knees yet revealed her milky calves. She wore a white blouse from which her delicate wrists shyly emerged. Her shiny hair was the color of corn and curly as a pig's tail. Her eyes were greener than young bamboo. Her smile engaged me. I was a squid ensnared in a fisherman's net. I followed her every word.

"The Bible, Acts 20:35 says: 'I had skewed you all things, how that so laboring ye ought to support the weak, and to remember the words of the Lord Jesus, how he said. It was more blessed to give than to receive.'"

She paused to let us absorb the strange concepts.

"We talked about this last week, do you remember, class?" She surveyed all 25 faces. Their eyes and mouths smiled equally.

While I beamed along with my classmates, she did not see my smile because I stared at my bare feet. I had no idea how to behave among regular people. I also had to hide my emotions.

Two other monks took this class. We had never met before. To respect their seniority, I refrained from speaking to them until they addressed me. They never did. I *wei*-ed to them, making sure to lower my head sufficiently. Half the students were women. This surprised me, but foreigners seemed to prefer unconventional classrooms. Even the State-run schools had less diversity than this one.

At the Baptist Student Center, people from foreign lands came to teach us English based on this book called the Bible. Miss Glover came from a country called Australia. She said Australia was the size of a lion and Thailand a kitten. The Center welcomed everyone—men and women—who had nowhere else to study. The others appeared indifferent to the fact that I wore a saffron robe. The class took place three afternoons a week. I attended this school because my alms rounds and *Pali* classes finished in the morning, leaving my afternoons free.

Miss Glover enunciated slowly: "Repeat after me, 'It is better to give than to receive.'"

After a long pause in which no one answered her, we parroted her words: "It is betta to give than to leceive."

"Good," she said, "but let's practice this word again." She rolled the r's and stretched the syllables.

"Rrr-e-ceive."

"Your tongue should go down instead of up." She pointed to her bottom teeth. We focused all our attention onto her mouth and listened to the sounds she made. I watched her without hearing her. I only saw her. Her lower lip reminded me of an orchid petal, delicate and bright.

"Rrre-cei-ve."

I said it with so much force that my voice rose above the others. I was a red jungle cock crowing louder than the roosters. Like wild birds that had been domesticated, I too had learned acceptable behavior. I had learned that I needed not to hunt for food to attract a hen in courtship, because none would have me anyway, with or without food, I fell to the bottom of the pecking order.

Miss Glover looked at me.

"Very good, *Phra* Amporn. Please repeat, for the class to hear you."

The way she pronounced my name created a warm feeling that I savored. Blood rushed to my face. I wished to disappear into the folds of my robe. I held my breath and dropped my head, but could not prevent my gaze from sneaking a peek to see whether she continued to look at me. Honeybees filled my stomach.

"Rrre-cei-ve," I repeated.

The effort from forcing my tongue behind my lower teeth caused my eyes to pop. I must have probably appeared ridiculous.

"Very good, *Phra* Amporn. You see, class, Thai people are capable of pronouncing the letter r-r," she purred with girlish enthusiasm.

"Try again. Move the tip of your tongue to your palate and say 'r-r-red.' "

Caught up in her spirit, we shouted out: "L-rr-ll-rr-ed."

Miss Glover turned toward me and nodded approvingly.

"Very good, class. See you on Wednesday." She stood up, signaling the class to do the same.

Unaccustomed to this, I rose last. At the temple, I was taught to *wei* to my teachers, to bend deeply in silence to show my respect. In this classroom, they expected me to stand up, look at my teacher, then say loudly: "Thank you, Miss Glover. See you on Wednesday."

I cursed myself for being so slow. I meant no disrespect to her. Even in Thai schools, students did not jump to their feet and shout out a greeting. This English ritual felt awkward and abrupt. At the temple, everything moved to the rhythm of elephants going uphill. The robes I wore set me apart from the world. Yet, when I stood with the other students, for that brief moment, the distance between us disappeared. I experienced a momentary pleasure. The abbot would have certainly disapproved.

I walked back to the temple, following the same old route. The new words from class, which I repeated out loud, fueled my steps. I kicked a stone to emphasize the syllables. The fat clouds rolled around. The afternoon heat fed my languidness.

Spotting the yellow flags ahead, my pace slowed. I tightened my robe. My head dangled like dried fruit on a branch. For a moment longer, I allowed myself to think of Miss Glover. She believed in a strange God that had transmitted His teachings in this book called the Bible. She glanced at the ceiling when she spoke of Him, as if He were there watching over her. She said His words were recorded in an ancient language that had been translated into English so everyone could read them. She prayed to Him every day. Her God believed in taking care of the poor. He had the power to send bad people to a place called hell, where they burned forever. Good people went to a place called heaven. In my mind I pictured a garden of orchids where the breeze blew gently. She said He created all people as equals. This confused me. If she looked around she would see a different truth. How was I an equal?

The temple gate cast its shadow upon me. At that moment I closed my eyes and forced my mind to empty itself. I left all thoughts of English, Miss Glover, and that other God outside the gates.

I played mental games. But forcing myself to think differently did not alter the reality. Still, I tried to fool myself. But at night, no matter how long I meditated, I could not control my thoughts. They meandered like ghosts who were wise to human trickery. The door ledges did not prevent them from slithering into the house at night, as I had been taught. Eventually, the bad ghosts learned how to avoid the good spirits guarding the family shrine by sneaking around to the back of the house, entering open windows and seeping through cracks in the wall.

My thoughts behaved similarly. They waited until I fell asleep to invade my dreams or wake me abruptly. I escaped the temple for any reason I could justify or explain. Still, at night I had to return. My *kutti* felt corked, the air stale. The cicadas were worn out by the heat and no longer bothered singing. The rooster awaited dawn. Abandoned cats wandered the temple grounds. In the dark, I forgot my resolve to keep Miss

Glover's words off the temple grounds. My skin drank up the humidity and swelled uncomfortably. Only my tongue had the will to move.

"You shall r-r-eap what you sow," I whispered, imagining a carp with bloated lips. I paused to reposition my tongue, and repeated the sentence.

My mind launched an attack: *You are a fake monk. Your Pali studies disinterest you, but learning English impassions you. Strangers paid for your robes to gain merit for their sick child. You took vows to train your mind, harness your thoughts, and travel the Noble Path. Instead you study English, frolic with females, and speak falsely to the abbot. Above all, you conjure fantasies of working in Bangkok, earning money, and having a family. You suffer from a strong ego. How many cursed lifetimes will you need before you learn humility?*

I reached for my earlobes and pinched them until they hurt. I wanted to wake up and take control of my thoughts. But I was not asleep. My mind raced. I clenched my teeth. I refused to think of her. She did not understand the Buddha, she did not believe in reincarnation, and she did not have the most beautiful smile. My mind recovered momentarily. I released my ears. As the pain faded, once again, her words rang in my head: "You shall reap what you sow."

The voice in my head shouted to frighten all the wandering ghosts: *And what shall that be?*

***

Stepping outside the temple gate one day, I saw another woman. My robe prohibited me from looking at women. I noticed her anyway. She wore her thick, black hair in a bun adorned with a bright yellow ribbon. Her brown eyes glimmered in the morning sun. I slowed down to admire her a bit longer.

When she noticed me she averted her eyes and gazed at the ground. Heat gathered in the small of my back. She lifted her head. Was I dreaming or did her eyelashes flutter? My face was the color of a sweet pepper. My pace quickened until I was safely out of her sight.

***

The abbot wore a disapproving expression.

"*Phra* Amporn, where have you been every other afternoon?" The loose skin from his bald head gathered on his forehead in a frown.

Overcome by nervousness, I felt the sweat pooling between my shoulders. I took a breath before answering.

"I have been studying, *Luang Por*."

"What have you been studying?"

"Languages."

"With other monks?"

"Yes, from two other temples."

"Very well."

"The only problem then is the young lady." His frown deepened.

"*Phra* Amporn, ever since you came to our temple, I was unsure whether you were of a noble heart in your intentions toward the *Sangha*. Still, you are the most earnest student I have ever known. You absorb everything quickly. You have learned to recite *Pali* verses with ease. You keep to yourself and cause no trouble with the others."

His face softened as he spoke.

"*Phra* Amporn, the robe is not a costume. It represents a way of life. It constitutes the path to self-realization and enlightenment. As cement and paint do not make a sculpture of the Buddha, saffron cloth may give you the external appearance of a monk but it does not make you one. You must dedicate yourself to the Noble Eightfold Path which, as you know, *Phra* Amporn, requires you to practice the 'right view'. You must regard the world the way it is, not the way you wish it to be. You must consider yourself the way you are, not the way you imagine yourself to be. What do you crave? What do you wish for that you can't obtain? The answer to these questions will reveal the causes of your suffering."

I remained closemouthed, distrusting the answers. I was, and had always been, a stupid boy with bad luck and a bad past. I wished to obtain a respectful job. I craved a family. For this I needed English, for I had no other skills. Yes, I suffered. I did not want to live in these robes for the rest of my life but I could not share these thoughts with him.

"*Phra* Amporn, you must use your efforts to abandon the 'wrong view', which arises from wrong speech, wrong action, and wrong mindfulness."

The abbot spoke in a tone just above the "right speech" way of the Noble Eightfold Path, which required speaking in a manner that reduced tension.

His words fueled my agitation. My head dropped to my chest. I struggled to hold on to my right speech. I squelched the words forming in my throat. I knew I had violated my vow of right intention, perhaps even on the very day of my ordination over a year ago.

"The time has come for you to choose, *Phra* Amporn. I give you one month to decide: the path instructed by the Buddha, or the path of the young lady who teaches English."

CHAPTER TWELVE

THE AROMA of green curry sauce wafted over the temple wall from the hut next door. It must have been intended for chicken. The perfume of coconut milk, green curry, eggplant, peas, kaffir lime leaves, and basil reached my nostrils. I pictured the family preparing the meal. A young mother runs her cleaver through the vegetables and meat on a worn, wooden block. Oil simmers in the pot. The woman watches over her small daughter who is chasing the family rooster. The baby brother totters after her, producing high-pitched giggles.

I imagined myself as the father into this scene. When I arrive home from work, my daughter spots me, abandons her chase, and runs to me with open arms. I lift her up and hold her aloft, a graceful heron. My son tugs at my trousers.

"Me, Papa! Me, Papa!" I place the squealing bird down, sweep up my little boy, and toss him into the air. Laughter erupts from his chubby tummy. My wife turns to me and winks. I belong among them.

I snapped at myself for entertaining such illusions. I stomp away from the temple to distance myself as much from the curry smells as from my fantasies.

The abbot said I had a choice. The Buddha said that for every situation there is a 'right action'. How could renouncing my vows be right? If I decided to leave the temple I would have to abandon my studies and would never get ahead. If I decided to stay, I would always be in the same place. I did not see how I had choices. The Buddha taught us that nothing whatsoever should be clung to for its own sake. I had no idea whether I should let go of my robes or my dreams.

My thoughts swirled. Like a merchant, I listed the benefits of staying in the robes: food given to me by strangers every day in exchange for my blessings, a bed at night, *Pali* and Buddhist studies for my mind, a sense of belonging to the monkhood, respect from everyone — and the knowledge that everything would be the same for the rest of my life. The sum of the positives impressed me. The negatives paled in comparison: dreams of having a job, a family, and a home.

Brooding all the way back to the temple, no closer to a decision, I almost walked into her. Each time I returned from my wanderings, she appeared and offered me water — the woman with the yellow ribbon in her hair whose beautiful eyes were forbidden to me.

She respected tradition and did not make eye contact with me. We had never exchanged a word but we had our water ritual. Each time, I offered her a blessing for her kindness. Each time, I noticed something new about her. I never minded pushing aside a *Pali* verse to remember the new discovery.

***

"I have decided to disrobe." Preferring to avoid the abbot's reaction, I examined my bare feet. Pride told me he had to experience a trace of sadness at my choice. When, at last, I raised my head, the abbot looked beyond me. Had I disappeared already? Did I ever matter? Was he meditating?

He fixed me in his gaze. For the first time, our eyes knew each other.

"You understand, don't you, *Luang Por*?" I had a sudden need for him to agree with me.

He reached over, placed his right hand on my bare, left shoulder, as if he was blessing me. He released my shoulder. "Where will you go?" he asked.

"I have no place to go."

"You may stay on the temple grounds for one more month, separate from the monks and novices. You must wear laymen's trousers and follow the appropriate precepts."

I nodded to acknowledge his kindness. Then I performed a *graab*, a full five-point prostration, to offer my gratitude.

***

The four monks sat next to the abbot chanting ancient texts intended for me. The chasm between us was as vast as the teachings themselves. Tradition required that I proclaim my change of status. I had to publicly and formally acknowledge that I renounced the life that had given life back to me. Did anyone here realize that? To stay within the robes would have been to abandon myself again.

The monks focused on the fly annoying the abbot, rather than on the ceremony. Disinterested in what this choice meant for me, they chanted at the appropriate times. They were traveling the road to personal enlightenment. The outside world expected nothing from them. They knew how to line up for the morning alms. Their rank and path were determined by their seniority. There was nothing else. They wore their robes with ease. They existed only for their internal journey.

As with everything on my path, my ceremony took place out of season. Normally, the disrobing ceremony only took place at the end of *pansa*, the rainy period. The novices who robed solely to make merit for their families returned to secular life at that time, to attend the new school term or, in some cases, to go back to work.

The abbot motioned me to come forward. I lowered my gaze, out of respect, but also to avoid seeing if the abbot carried any disappointment toward me. My ego still wished to know that he had held expectations of me. I knew I could neither forsake nor camouflage my desires for a family and a home. No matter how tightly I tied the knot that secured my robes, I had always known it would eventually come loose.

I, *Phra* Amporn, took one last breath before returning to my former self, Lek.

"*Phra* Amporn, do you have anything you wish to say?"

For days I had contemplated how to explain why I was leaving the brotherhood of monks.

"*Luang Por*, I ask forgiveness for any offenses I may have committed while in the monkhood. After much thinking, I have chosen to return to the status of layman. I wish to continue my English studies."

I had given him the simplest answer.

The abbot nodded in a slow, deliberate manner, as if to give me a moment to reconsider.

Silence.

"I understand your intentions."

Another pause.

I examined his face for clues as to his feelings. I detected none. He focused on the ritual, which had no personal significance for him, and continued.

"Once you leave the *Sangha*, you will be addressed by your given name, Mr. Amporn Wathanavongs, using the layman's title, *Khun* Amporn. You are no longer bound by your 227 vows."

My heart unlocked. Lek stepped out. In my own mind, I silently addressed my mother: *Mommy, Mommy, I am back. Please do not be upset. I want a family like you had. I want my straw hat to hang on a hook beside the door, like father's did.* I knew what stirred in my heart. The time had come to create a respectable man out of myself.

I wanted to skip away the moment the abbot paused, but the ceremony was not over. Before his last words, my attention had shifted to that place just outside the temple gate where I had seen the woman wearing the yellow ribbon so many times. In my imagination she waited for me.

The abbot frowned. I realized I had allowed my head to rise. He had seen the peacock peeking out of his robe. I sensed his disapproval and wanted the ceremony to end. I had chosen.

"Do you accept to continue to honor the Five Basic Precepts of the layperson?" he asked.

"Yes, I promise to abstain from taking life, from intoxicants, from sexual misconduct, from false speech, and from taking what is not given."

Once more I prostrated myself before the abbot. Six years had passed since I had worn trousers. I could read and write. I was no longer a boy; I was a man. I turned around and walked into the world, hungry to meet life, not death.

***

Freed from my robes on a beautiful spring day, I walked about the village to look for work. My first day as a layperson coincided with Coronation Day. King Bhumibal Adulyadig had been coroneted nine years before, on May 5, 1950. Because it was a public holiday, the children were released from the boredom of attending State school classes. They wandered through the village playing games. A sense of anticipation filled the air. On such occasions, traveling shows could appear without warning.

The rumor of a shadow puppet show had been slithering from town to town on a snake's back. For days, villagers passing through neighboring towns had been saying that they had heard distant sounds like those of the theater and *nora* masters, a performance tradition blending dance, drama, and ritual.

Villagers in southern Thailand, where *nora* masters usually performed, loved this form of entertainment. Excitement built all day long. Typically, the troupe arrived before sunset to set up their screens. Because the shows opened after dark and lasted until dawn, the children were permitted to stay up late. Their younger brothers and sisters fell asleep in their laps while the parents socialized behind them. A few of the men were brave enough, or silly enough, to smoke.

People ignored me. Without my robes, I was an ordinary-looking man. At times I thought I saw a hint of recognition. Given the commotion accompanying the festivities, no one looked at me long enough to identify me. They knew me, but they did not. A few waved without offering the traditional *wei*.

I circled the temple, like a nestling scared to leave its nest. I knew what I wanted in life. At this particular juncture, I craved to be part of the village and enjoy the shadow puppet show. Usually they performed *Jatakas*, tales that recounted the previous lives of *Bodhisattva*, as animal, god, mendicant, or king. Always the story expressed some virtues to which we should aspire. I loved to listen to these tales; they filled me with hope.

That night the master had selected the *Munika-Jataka*, the story of the ox who envied the pig. I had heard this one before. It was the story of a former monk. After he disrobed, life became more difficult for him, and he longed for the comforts of the temple: food, shelter, and studying. While considering a return to the monastery, he encountered a master who told him the story of the *Bodhisattva*, who was born as an ox named Big Red. He and his younger brother, Little Red, performed all the farm work, pulled the family cart and plowed the fields. They were fed straw and grass for their hard work. The family's pig spent his days rolling in the mud. The pig was fed rice and, sometimes, leftover curry. He grew fat and was slaughtered for a daughter's marriage feast.

The message, the master puppeteer reminded the villagers at the end of the performance, was that in this unpredictable life, living humbly and eating simply leads to a good life that would not be cut short. At that point, the puppets were barely visible in the dawn light. Many villagers had already returned to their huts.

The tale resonated as if it had been written for me. If my mother were alive, she would have chosen this very story for me that night. I had a new life. I vowed to make it simple so it was not cut short. How to do so puzzled me in the same way ancient riddles mystified me.

With no one in sight, I kicked the first stone I saw with all my might, to propel us both into my future. No longer a monk, I could skip. I shouted a big "*Ka!* Yes!" that had been lying dormant for many years. My voice was strong.

"*Ka*! Yes!" I repeated again and again because I could. My voice traveled in the direction of the rising sun. I laughed, releasing the joy of my hopes for the future, until my stomach ached.

"I am *Khun* Amporn," I roared. With this cry, I was born into my new life.

CHAPTER THIRTEEN

I DROPPED the long, steel machete with some other tools at the edge of the golf course.

"Should I come back tomorrow?" I asked *Khun* Jaet.

"No, Amporn. Work is done, come back next week. Maybe more work then. Wait. I get you money."

"*Kob kun krap*. Thank you." I *wei*-ed bending deeper than required. It was enough to flatter the man. All the tricks I picked up in the markets of Surin years ago had resurfaced. When a hunter returns to the jungle after a long absence, his survival instincts kick in the second he faces a python.

My intentions went beyond wheedling my way into his good graces for more work. I had other motives. I had discovered that *Khun* Jaet was the father of Sunee, the woman in yellow ribbons who used to give me water outside the temple. But something strange happened. After I disrobed, she disappeared for a few days.

It had been silly of me to fabricate a story in which she might consider me a man rather than a monk. I realized she had been bound by her belief in doing good deeds in this life, to earn a better one next time. She had seen my robe that was all. Every morning she had been the one appointed to make merit for her family. Usually, family members took turns. I had let my imagination create something more of her kindness than was warranted. She had respected the saffron cloth in which I had been hiding. I had been otherwise invisible to her. But she had been visible to me.

While *Khun* Jaet went to fetch my pay, I sat under a mango tree recalling the day good fortune had come to me. Early one morning about two weeks after I last saw her, I left the temple to search for work. There she was again, the woman who brought me water daily, tending to an elderly man leaning against a fence. The man looked ill.

"*Sawadee*. Good morning. Is this man sick? Do you need help?" I asked.

"This is my father," she said. "He is unwell. He has missed many days of work. I am worried he will lose his job." Her eyes filled with tears.

I wondered if she recognized me.

"*Khun*..." My voice trailed off as I realized that I did not know her name.

"*Nong* Sunee," she said.

I did not know why she referred to herself as *Nong*, little sister, but I was afraid to ask her.

"Yes, *Nong* Sunee, so many times you have quenched my thirst when I was returning to the temple. I am *Khun* Amporn. You may not recognize me without my robe. May I return your kindness? May I accompany your father to his work?"

We spoke with the familiarity of people who had met a long time ago.

"I think he may be too ill," she said. "It would be so kind if you went to his work — my father cuts grass at the golf course up the road — and told his boss that he sent you to replace him until he feels better. If that would be acceptable." Her gaze traveled to my hands.

I shoved them into my trouser pockets, hiding their softness and my sudden shame. The only manual labor I had done in recent years had been to sweep the temple grounds.

"I will be happy to do so."

I nodded and headed for the golf course. Our conversation played in my mind with the exuberance of wild monkeys.

Khun Jaet returned, interrupting my daydreaming. He handed me exactly 13 *baht*, enough for one bowl of noodles each day for two weeks.

"*Khun* Amporn. Sorry, no more work fo' you. You do good. You come my house tomorrow for supper. My daughter, *Khun* Sunee, she cook for us." He winked at me before walking away.

***

I set out for my two hour walk back to the temple. After eight hours of backbreaking work cutting grass, my feet could not bear the weight of my sandals. I should have been grateful that *Khun* Jaet found me work at another golf course, even though it was farther away.

Morning was his worst enemy. He preferred nighttime and beer for company.

Everything irritated me on that day. Since my time in the jungle, I had managed to avoid using a machete. Calluses covered my hands from the manual labor. They had become rough and ugly. My spine had aged 30 years in a few weeks. My straight posture from years of meditation was no longer. My skin had grown pale and fragile from so many hours of studying. Even the alms round had taken place before sunrise. In spite of the straw hat I wore when working, the sun had cooked me into a dark shade of brown. I had forgotten what it was like to be poor, hungry, and without shelter. The thought that I would soon be homeless again gnawed at me worse than lice. I could not ask the abbot for more time. While stray dogs could stay indefinitely at the temple, I had an expiration date.

I distracted myself by thinking of *Nong* Sunee. This term of endearment had been unfamiliar to me until she introduced herself. At first, I took it to mean she liked me as a brother. My years studying *Pali* had left me with no knowledge about women. When I asked a man on the golf course the meaning of "little sister," he poked me in the ribs and said, "She likes you. You special."

I slapped his arm to show appreciation for his humor. I must have used too much force. He stepped back and rubbed his arm.

"I'm sorry, *Khun* Pichat," I said. "You tickled me." I lied, of course, but it was a simple lie, the kind permitted to laymen.

Every day, hour after hour, I cut grass. I overcame boredom by thinking of Sunee. My thoughts hovered around this exquisite flower, waiting for the right moment to taste her sweetness. Every day when I went to and from work, we waved to each other. I told myself it must mean something. Some evenings, when her father watched over his beer, she came out to offer me water again.

I coaxed my feet to keep moving forward, distracting myself from my exhaustion by remembering the instant our eyes had met. We had our own private language, talking to each other through furtive glances. When we felt brave, our eyes lingered on one another. This was no longer reprehensible. I wore trousers now. Her eyes, like raindrops on a banana leaf in the morning sun, mesmerized me. Waves of excitement surged through my body. I tingled, savoring this new and pleasurable sensation. When she stepped closer, the sensation intensified. How could I explain this? Perhaps I was nervous in the presence of women.

I was searching for the words to speak my heart to *Nong* Sunee. In my imagination, we had held long conversations while the moon rose. I had visualized touching her hand and had rehearsed the scene to perfection. The fantasy started to take shape, getting more familiar to me and becoming more possible with each hour I spent doing dull, repetitive work on the golf course. In one daydream, I told her of my plans to marry her, learn English, and get an important job in Bangkok. We had our own hut. Then we had children. In this daydream, which I directed, she blushed. Someday, I would turn that imaginary scene into reality.

If I paced myself, I had enough water in my gourd for the walk back. After seven kilometers, the countryside bled into urbanity. When I approached the slums, my pace slowed. Bright red, yellow, and pink sarongs hung out to dry outside a dull patchwork of corrugated steel roofs, bamboo stilts, and coarse dust. The shanties had their own rhythm. The songs were composed of languid notes resting on tired bones. A father napped between back-to-back shifts in Bangkok. A mother paused to wipe her brow and readjusted the child tied snugly onto her back. A grandmother dragged herself from the rice fields to home. Only the children skipped along; they did not yet know they were poor. Nourished by the love they received, they waved to passersby with all the energy of well-fed youngsters.

I reminisced as I fondled the coins in my pocket in the same manner I used to finger my chanting beads. When I was a monk, it took only one hour to fill my alms bowl to the rim. And there would be enough left over to share with some of the novices. Then, I was free to study all day. I realized that it now took me eight hours of cutting, trimming, and shaving every blade of grass on an 18-hole golf course to the standards required by the Bangkok elite to earn enough money to buy one meal a day. When I disrobed, I promised to abstain from taking what was not given freely. I worked for my food and refused to steal again. I willed myself to put one foot in front of the other and keep walking.

I noticed a small wooden structure, a bit sturdier, a bit more conspicuous than the houses in the village. The sign in front read: "French Catholic Jesuit Center." I sounded it out, remembering the English alphabet from class, but I had no idea what it meant. I missed those lessons. *Damn bad luck.* I looked around to make sure no one had heard my thoughts. Old habits resurfaced daily. It angered me when it happened. I wanted the old ways to be buried forever.

The Thai inscription made no sense to me: *Soon Klang Tewa*-Angel Center. No one was about. In one window, a small light burned. I gave into my curiosity. I dragged my weary legs up each step. I stood at the door and examined the wooden walls. I wondered if perhaps they would reveal to me what was inside. I listened for voices. Hearing nothing, I pushed open the door.

A foreign-looking man in a long, white dress with reading glasses perched on the tip of his nose stood before me. He looked up and removed his glasses. I gazed into ocean-blue eyes. His expression was neither threatening nor friendly. We surveyed one another. I considered turning around and rushing down the stairs but I was too tired. It was much cooler in there.

"Bonjour, *Sawadee. Je suis Père Bonningue.* I am Father Bonningue," the man said in broken Thai

"Hello," I blurted. It was the only foreign greeting I knew. The man spoke in another foreign language.

"*Sawadee,*" I said, to find common ground.

He looked perplexed. Certain I had done wrong, I looked down. Something was familiar about this language. I had heard it before. But where? In the jungle. My legs trembled. I wanted to run. Fear pulsed through me. Sweat poured down my face and dripped onto my neck.

Behind the man, an open door led to another room. I peered into it, looking for signs of danger. The sight of row upon row of books overwhelmed me.

He led me into that other room, pulled up a chair and gestured for me to sit down.

"Are you thirsty? How about a glass of water? You look quite pale."

I nodded.

When he left, I rushed over to examine the books. Many were in Thai, but most were in foreign languages. I wondered how many were in English. Surrounded by books, my breathing slowed. My eyes flitted from volume to volume and recorded the colorful mosaic of the covers.

When he returned, I realized the man with the kind expression was a full head taller than I. His reading glasses rested on the bald spot above his fringe of white hair. He moved gracefully, in a gentle and nonthreatening way. The white dress undulated gently around him. His gaze was undemanding and unquestioning. He placed his oversized hands on the large blue book he placed in front of me.

"Would you be interested in learning to read?" he asked in Thai.

"I can read," I said in defense of my shabby appearance. "I mean, I can read *Pali* and Thai," I quickly added.

He caressed the book with a caring familiarity.

"I love to read." I wanted to convince him that my love of books equaled his.

Silence.

He was in no rush. I wondered why he was wearing a white dress.

"I want to learn to read English. Do you have English books?"

"*Kap*. Yes. Would you like to come and read our books?"

I had to think about it.

"Yes."

I could barely keep still. I wanted to talk to him. And I was scared we would be interrupted. Ever since I left Miss Glover's class to find work, I had worried that I would never again have a chance to study English.

"What do I need to do to be able to read your English books?"

"Come and visit whenever you have time."

Although he spoke in Thai, I did not understand his answer. Was he suggesting I take classes there? I did not want to appear stupid, so I did not ask for an explanation; instead I changed the subject.

"What does it mean, Catholic Jesuit Center?" The second I opened my mouth I realized I had exposed my inability to speak English — and my ignorance.

"Well, we call it the Angel Center. You Thai people believe in ghosts. Angels are good ghosts; they help guide us. We are here to teach poor children, to be guardian angels for them. People from our French Embassy who speak Thai come on Sundays and teach the children to read and write so they can have a better life."

I nodded. This I understood. The words tumbled out.

"Do you teach English too? What if I do not live in the area? Am I too old to be a child? What must I do?"

The man laughed.

"Yes, we do teach English. We bring people from other embassies to help. We also show English films to the adults. Yes, you look older than a child." He smiled again.

This could not have been another Baptist Center, or he would have mentioned the Bible. I wanted him to approve of me. I wanted to avoid annoying him with too many questions, but I was confused about the nature of the place.

"Really? Anyone can come and study English here?"

A chortle rose from deep in his belly, causing his dress to ripple. I did not understand what was so funny.

"Yes, anyone can come. You have so many questions, young man. Do you live around here?"

"It is a two hour walk. Soon I'll live closer. I am moving in three weeks."

"What does Jesuit mean?" I wanted to distract him from asking too many questions. They might have led to the wrong answers.

"A group of people in France who help pay for this center."

"Are you part of the Baptist churches?"

"No. We belong to a large Christian family called Catholics. We are different."

"I am confused. You are one religion, but different. Do you have the same Bible?"

He smiled, transmitting kindness instead of contempt. I liked that I amused him.

"What is your name?"

Why was he changing the subject?

"I am Amporn Wathanavongs."

I wanted to say, "Pleased to meet you." I remembered this salutation vaguely from English class. But the words remained stuck in my throat. In the temple, robes commanded a silent *wei*, not words.

"Pleased to meet you. My name is Père Bonningue. I am a priest in the Catholic Church."

"Are you Mr. Père or Mr. Bonningue?" My tongue twirled around those strange syllables.

"I am a priest. Our roles are different from monks in Buddhism. My name would translate to '*Phra* Bonningue,' except in France we say '*Père*,' which means 'Father.'"

I kept to myself that I had recently left the robes. Based on what I saw, priests and monks were very different. If I asked for more explanations, he may have thought of me as uneducated.

"*Sawadee*, Père Bonningue," I said. I wanted to impress him with my learning skills.

"Very good." His shoulders jiggled up and down. "You are good with languages, I see."

"Are priests and monks the same?"

"That's a long conversation for some other time."

He must have noticed that I was staring at his robe.

"I wear a white frock. Monks wear saffron robes. In my country, depending on which group of priests you belong to, you wear a different color. It is simpler in Thailand where all the monks wear the same color. I am happy with my white robe. It matches my hair. I do not think I would look good in orange."

A chuckle escaped before I could catch it. Either it was a strange religion or he was a strange man. He made me laugh and he liked to talk. He smiled. He chuckled. I did the same. We were two chattering parrots. When we laughed together, we joined in a communion greater than any moment I had ever experienced at the temple. Except, perhaps, for the night *Phra* Teacher and I had spoken.

"I am glad you stopped by. I like you, young man."

"*Kob kun krap*. Thank you, *Père* Bonningue. I will come again soon."

"Please do, *Khun* Amporn."

I left the Angel Center and headed for *Nong* Sunee's home. I skipped along to a new rhythm. I hoped that maybe that night I would find the words to speak to her.

CHAPTER FOURTEN

WHEN THE meal ended, Sunee's father handed me a surprise. He left us alone under the pretense of fetching water.

Sunee spoke first.

"*Khun* Amporn, my father say you come live with us. He say you work very hard at the golf course. He say he no want you to move to downtown Bangkok, that be too far to work for him. He say he no have to pay you so much like other men because you fast." *Nong* Sunee said in one breath and without looking at me.

"A very generous offer, *Nong* Sunee. Your father is a very kind man. And your mother too, of course. I, I …"

My mind raced to figure out how to answer. I wanted to say yes. It would solve all my problems. And I would be close to Sunee. What would *Khun* Jaet expect of me? Would I have to replace him at work every time he drank too much beer and could not get up in the morning? I could manage. If I had to, I could do the work at my other job at night.

Still, I worried. I had lived alone since I was five. I had learned how to behave around other monks, but had no idea how to live with a family. The thought of seeing Sunee everyday made the blood rush to my face. My cheeks burned and turned the shade of watermelon.

Sunee fidgeted with her skirt, tracing the circles in the fabric, maybe to memorize the pattern.

"You can sleep in our kitchen," she said. "It's nicest-smelling part of house. My mother, she says OK too."

"I would be honored to live with your family. *Kob kun krap*. Thank you. Please tell your father and mother that I accept. I will come in two days. I take only a little space. I can sleep anywhere. I will help with household chores, I—"

Nong Sunee squealed. I commanded my face to remain serious and composed. Embarrassment mixed with relief lingered on her forehead. For the first time, I noticed she had bangs. She parted them in the middle and drew them apart like curtains. I smiled. I wanted to discover more about her.

She looked straight at me, daring me to meet her gaze. Her expression relaxed, and she giggled, a nervous, girlish laughter.

Did it mock me or reveal her delight? I listened more carefully. The sound swelled into pleasure. A tingling sensation overtook me, like drinking a steaming cup of coconut milk on a cold, rainy day. Heat surged through me. Perhaps someone had dropped hot, chili peppers into the drink. Life tasted so delicious, I wanted to hold on to it forever. We laughed.

***

Sunee moved across the kitchen floor, her footsteps like those of a sparrow. I recognized her sweet rhythm. Stretched out on a faded bamboo mat in the kitchen, I pretended to sleep. I waited for the moment when Sunee left the hut. When the moon had changed places with the sun, I watched her shadow cross to a bench behind the house, under the teak tree. She performed a personal ritual. First, while squatting before it, she wiped the sagging planks with her right hand and then turned to sit. She kicked off her sandals, stretched her arms over her head, closed her eyes, and shook her head gently from side to side to release the tension in her neck. Her arms dropped to her thighs; she took a deep breath and leaned against the tree. She looked up at the sky. Then — and this was my favorite part — she smiled. Her teeth shined so white, they rivaled the brightness of the moon. Her body sank and her head dropped to the side in a meditative trance. The stars must have answered her questions. Tranquility transformed her face.

I loved that stolen time with her. She may have been unaware that I observed her but I cherished those private moments with her. Behind her parents' backs, we had furtive exchanges, a few specks of intimacy in a shared glance or the brush of a sleeve. That night, the sight of her tortured me. My body ached to be next to her on the bench. It was if her appearance dared me to do something.

The attraction intensified to the point that it became intolerable. I had to travel the space separating our two universes. I got up and crept like a cat toward her. My steps more closely resembled those of a baby elephant and I tripped over the door ledge. *Stupid ghosts*, I cursed silently. My heart froze.

Her face hardened, her smile disappeared. She looked around to see what had interrupted her communion with the stars. When she saw me, her shoulders relaxed. She straightened her sarong and placed her hands on the bench. I looked at the softness of her fingers curled around the rough edges of the wood. She leaned forward. I took this as a nod from fate and tiptoed closer. Her smile broadened. As I moved closer, she hid behind her long bangs.

I panicked. Had I come too close? I sat next to her, leaving enough space for a rice bowl.

"You cannot sleep, *Nong* Sunee?" I whispered.

"I like the dark, the quiet, and the stars — my peace time to sit here every evening by myself."

"I know." I swallowed. *Stupid, stupid me*. She would know that I had been watching her. To hide my self-hatred, I looked down. My inner voice assaulted me with recriminations.

She responded the way she always did, covering her mouth with her right hand and giggling.

Her reaction made my heart dance. I felt dizzy, a puppet to my emotions. I placed my right hand over her left hand. The touch bewitched me. Every nerve in my body thrilled. I moved my other hand to her shoulder.

Sunee's head rose. I moved closer. Her eyes had a hint of honey. I felt the warmth of her breath as she exhaled. My lips found hers. The moistness of her mouth, the jasmine of her skin, and the tickle of her hair teased my manhood. My resistance collapsed when our tongues met.

Sunee, the woman, not the little sister, reposed against the tree and closed her eyes. I retreated to my blanket in the kitchen and drifted off to sleep.

***

"Bonjour, *sawadee*, *Khun* Amporn."

I recognized his voice.

"You will wear out our table if you keep rubbing English letters into the wood with your finger."

Father Bonningue sat across from me. I had been studying an English language book for many, many hours.

"*Sawadee*. I don't think so. I erase the letters every day before I leave."

I enjoyed how we played with words together.

"I am making much progress. I have memorized the entire alphabet."

"Already?"

"Yes. But I find it a strange language. Why do they have two letters that sound the same?"

"Which ones?"

"The letters 'l' and 'r'. Why do *farang*, foreign, things have to be so complicated?"

Father Bonningue's shoulders shook. I prepared myself for the laugh I knew would follow.

"*Je ne sais pas*. I don't know. It is English, after all."

We shared the same struggles as *farang* speakers of that capricious language. He spent the next half hour teaching me words starting with "l" and "r." He showed me how to position my tongue against the roof of my mouth to produce a correct "r."

"Rrred, rrroof, rrroad," I repeated.

"Now relax your tongue and let it drop to the bottom of our mouth. Repeat after me: 'Llletter, llllittle, lllemon.'"

He laughed harder when I pronounced the "l."

"See you on Sunday when Miss Desirrrrrre will teach her English class," he said. The "r" rolled over the nearby fields.

He patted me on the head, unaware that in my culture he had exhibited bad manners, and floated away. I no longer minded when he touched my head or laughed at my pronunciation. I cherished the familiarity growing between us. Some things still perplexed me: his robe fostered our friendship instead of separating us. He seemed to want to understand me, not only guide me. How much warmer his Christian faith was than my Buddhist teachings.

I settled back into my chair for another hour of studying. Practicing "r" the way Father Bonningue had taught me, I tried too hard and spat on the page. How my life had changed since I had left the robes. I was starring in my own life rather than drifting from one sad song to another.

I had been living with Sunee's family for two weeks. Sunee and I had kissed a week ago. Every day since, we had met on the bench under the watchful gaze of the setting moon and rising sun. Each time we sat closer, until she allowed me to hold her.

I had yet to find the courage to speak of my future dreams. I did not want to spoil our sweet embraces. But I knew that someday I would have to. Then I would ask her to marry me. First, I needed a better job that paid more money. I needed to rent us a small home. *Khun* Pook would be my mother-in-law and *Khun* Jaet would be my father-in-law.

The thought of *Khun* Jaet angered me. Without Sunee saying a word, I saw how he frightened her. I had seen his hand raised in anger before he slammed it on the table. She flinched but kept silent. I understood why her mother spent so much time away from the house, escaping to the fields, the market, or the yard. Sunee would feel safe with me. He could not find out that we had kissed. With a few Chang beers in his stomach, who knew how he would react? He might throw me out or forbid Sunee to speak to me. She would never disobey her father.

Stupid me, I cursed myself. I had to stop thinking in the old way. I should not be thinking of the bad outcomes all the time. Things were going well. I could worry about my bad *karma* later, in my next life. I would have plenty of time after reincarnation. I needed to dwell on good things. I focused on Father Bonningue and his kindness toward me. He helped me to learn English. When he laughed, I thought nothing could go wrong.

He showed me an image in a Bible. A man wore the same white dress as his and carried a long, curly stick for guiding sheep. That day I learned the words "shepherd" and "flock." I had a hard time pronouncing the "l" in flock. Father Bonningue said sometimes he had problems with his flock too. Then he laughed. It made me think of *Phra* Teacher and how serious he was when I was studying the Buddha's teachings with him.

I loved Sundays. I listened to Father Bonningue say "Mass" in yet another *farang* language. He called it Latin, a dead language because no one speaks it. I thought he enjoyed it, too, this "Mass" ritual. He looked so calm, smiling at the people, holding up his arms, ready to embrace everyone. I loved it when he made the sweeping gesture of bringing his hands together. It told me he welcomed all of us. Anyone could attend.

The ceremony lasted about an hour. Afterward, he stayed to answer questions. He told me his God had a son named Jesus. The one in the picture, the shepherd I had seen in the Bible. Father Bonningue said if you prayed and asked for forgiveness, God had the power to absolve you of your sins. His God must have been only for *farang*. People like me who had lived in the markets and the jungle had too many sins. We were Thai. We had to come back again and again to correct our mistakes until we got it right. According to the Buddha's teachings, only then would we have had a better life. I preferred the Buddha's way. Who wanted to burn forever in hell? I thought that was inhumane. I also wondered why believers did not simply ask for forgiveness and go to heaven. Next time I saw Father Bonningue, I would ask him.

That time of day had come for me to put away the book that I had been studying and go home. Sunee was going to cook her magic that night. Her mother preferred tending to the garden. Sunee hummed while turning a pot of steaming carrots, peas, and bamboo shoots into a flavorful dish to tickle my palate. In her hands *nam pla* — fish sauce — *galangal*, and dried herbs from her mother's garden mixed to create meals far better than any food stall. She was relaxed in the kitchen, just like my mother was.

***

"You skinny, dark monkey. You came to my home two weeks ago, you sleep in my kitchen, and you think you can steal my daughter. I'm going to kill you dead," *Khun* Jaet yelled, and waved the axe he used to chop wood.

The only thing that kept me and Sunee from being dismembered was the tired kitchen table.

"Please, *Khun* Jaet, please put the axe down so we can talk. Why are you so upset? I do not want to offend you in any way."

I spoke slowly. I needed time to think.

When *Khun* Jaet placed a hand on the table to steady himself, he knocked over five empty beer bottles. They rattled between us.

"Shit," he said.

"*Khun* Jaet, you are a kind man offering me your home," I said. "I respect your daughter. I would do nothing to harm her."

"Liar. I see you go out of the house in the night. I see she gone. I no stupid." He downed another mouthful of beer.

"Daddy, please. I only go outside to get fresh air when I cannot sleep."

"Shut up. You no talk back to me."

He raised his bottle over her head. Sunee flinched. I realized he had probably performed this gesture many times before.

"Shut up. You no good girl. First you kiss that monkey, then you with baby. I know."

I forced Sunee behind me at the same time I pushed against the table to create a barrier between her father and us. The bottles crashed to the floor. I looked up at *Khun* Jaet. His anger had transformed into rage. Too drunk to hold onto the bottle in his hand, he dropped it on top of the others, where it shattered.

I grabbed the broken bottle with my left hand, waved it near his face, and shot him a defiant look. With my bad right hand I took hold of Sunee's hand. She stood behind me, shivering, half-crying, and too scared to move. I turned to face her. Our eyes met. I had to protect her from this drunken thug.

"Sunee, we have to leave. Your father will harm us. Please come with me. I promise, I will find a way to take care of you. If you stay here, I fear for what he will do to you. I care about you. You must decide right now." The words marched from my mouth as if they had been trained for this moment.

I saw pain on her face. I prayed for my words to reach her heart. I had dreamed of leaving with her, but not like this.

She nodded. I squeezed her hand.

"We are leaving now, *Khun* Jaet. I am taking Sunee with me. You will not hurt her anymore. I will take care of her."

Holding the jagged bottle, our only defense, in front of me, I led Sunee to the door. I stood between her and her father, who was saturated with alcohol and anger. Never before had I had the courage to hold another man's stare. We fixated on each other, two tigers circling, waiting to pounce.

"Leave now, you snake. Both of you. Sunee, you bad girl. No come crawling to me later.

You take her, you poo' bastard. One less mouth fo' me to feed. Go, or I chop you to pieces and feed them to dogs."

Sunee walked out of her childhood home. I would keep her safe. I left my loneliness with *Khun* Jaet. I had no more need for it.

CHAPTER FIFTEEN

"*SAWADEE KHUN* Amporn. How is my faithful reading companion today?" said Father Bonningue, whose voice traveled into the library of the Angel Center, where I was reading a dictionary. He stood in the doorway.

"*Sawadee*, Father Bonningue. Very good. I continue to progress in my English class. I wish I could come more often."

"Why don't you?"

"I don't have much time to myself. I have to look for more work. It takes a lot of time. Last year, I lived with *Khun* Jaet in exchange for regular work at the golf course. I want to learn English quickly so I can get a better job. I have *Khun* Sunee to take care of."

I rubbed my forehead to release the tension I felt whenever I thought about cutting grass for the rest of my life.

Father Bonningue took a step and shut the door behind him. He had never done that before. What trouble awaited me?

"*Khun* Amporn, what kind of work would interest you?"

"Any respectable work. I must first speak English very good, so—"

He interrupted with his usual smile. "Very well."

"Yes, very well." Wanting to express myself clearly, I switched to Thai. Over the last few months, our conversations had become a mix of Thai and English. I thought his name should have been Saint Patience.

"Father Bonningue, I want to have an office job in Bangkok. I haven't figured out what they do in the offices, but they walk with their heads high. Once I speak fluently, I will find work with what they call a company. I want to wear a suit. I want people to listen to me. I want to find a real house for *Khun* Sunee and me to live in."

"Where do you live now?"

"A family rents us the space under their stilt house for 50 *baht* each month. *Khun* Sunee possesses much courage. She never complains about the mosquitoes or the cold. She just snuggles up to me." *Uh-oh*. It slipped out. I now avoided eye contact. I did not mean to say what I was thinking. Sunee curled up like a kitten in my arms on cold nights. The warmth of our united bodies provided me with the greatest pleasure I had ever known.

Father Bonningue had taken vows of chastity. I renounced mine. Banished were the long nights of solitude when my body longed for companionship. I used to engage in monologues, which usually ended in negotiation with imaginary ghosts. I plead to be reborn a husband – a cause I knew to be futile, as I was destined for rebirth as a worm or some other low creature.

Sunee's body had become my relief from the pain of chopping grass, blade by blade, with a stubby, rusted machete. When her hair tickled my nose, or when I inhaled her scent (which I later believed to be mine), I prayed that I did not barter with some devilish spirits. I feared I would have to pay for those momentary pleasures, which I had not earned. In those moments, my veins coursed with rebelliousness where submissiveness used to flow. The loneliness that tied me into knots had transformed into a brutish force. I wanted to save Sunee, above all. She held the way to my future, to my family.

For those two months, when we lay cocooned, I thirsted to hold her tight enough to fold into me. I waited for her to drift off, the delicious moment when her mind released all its worries and her body welcomed rest. I allowed my left hand to rest on her belly, where she carried our first child. I held that baby from its first breath. I caressed all my family at once.

Father Bonningue coughed lightly. "Are you still with me?" he asked.

I hoped the redness of my face camouflaged my thoughts. I nodded, unwilling to trust my tongue. It had a habit of betraying me.

"How long have you been living in this way?" he asked.

Did he mean in sin or without a proper house? I wondered if he would disapprove of my living with a woman outside of matrimony. I doubted he would approve of Sunee and me having a family now, before we married. He must have known poor people lacked the means to pay for a formal ceremony. However, having a child out of wedlock touched the nerves attached to the sanctity of procreation.

"Almost a year."

"*Khun* Amporn?" Father Bonningue raised his voice.

"*Kap*. Sorry, Father Bonningue, I was thinking of the last year. I have been trying … very hard to …"

"*Je sais*. I know, *Khun* Amporn. I have something to ask you."

"Yes?"

"The Angel Center needs to hire someone to help with many chores."

"What chores?"

"Keep our books organized in the library, sweep the floors, clean the toilets, and sometimes accompany the children to and from their homes for the morning classes. They come for the bowl of rice we give them after the reading and writing classes. We pray that they'll learn a little too, have a better chance in life. But mostly, they come to eat."

I nodded. What did this have to do with me? Maybe someone complained and Father Bonningue no longer wished to grant me use of the library. Maybe I had bothered him too much with questions and he needed to ask me to leave him alone. I could not imagine a life without learning.

"Since my Thai is rough and you have proven very reliable, I thought I might hire you. Would you accept working here at the Angel Center?"

Without care for my impoliteness, my jaw dropped. I was frozen in disbelief.

"It doesn't pay very much, but it would be regular. You and *Khun* Sunee could live here. When the Center closes at night, it could be your home."

My tongue refused to form a single syllable.

"She could cook behind the Center, with everyone else during the day."

I looked from his lips to the books crowding the shelves. I could be responsible for all of those. I could listen to all the English classes. I could …

"*Khun* Amporn, you would work for me. Do you want me to be your boss? I can be very demanding at times."

He winked.

"*Kap*. Yes. *Kap*. Yes."

I hopscotched between languages. I had secured my first real job. I imagined Sunee pumping her arms overhead with delight. She would find the nearest Ganesh shrine and make an offering. Our first child would be born to a working father. Our child would go to school and the family would travel a road to a better life.

"Come here with *Khun* Sunee tomorrow at the end of the day. We will talk about the details."

Father Bonningue wore a schoolboy's grin. He patted me on the shoulder and then left the room, singing to himself in French.

I had a job!

***

It had become our routine. I roused Sunee from her sleep. I could barely make out the rising sun. Sunee turned to our baby son, Theerachai, whom we had nicknamed Piak, lying next to her. Lifting his naked body, she sleepwalked down the stairs to lie in the hammock under a mosquito net. There she fed him. Mother and son swung back and forth between their dreams and the early moments of the day. I observed them from the window in the library as I had for the last year. I could have watched them all day and night and never tired of it.

I rolled up the straw mat, the blankets and pillows still drenched with my family's warmth, and stored the bundle behind a cabinet.

I knew from the moment Father Bonningue offered me the job, we would sleep there. I joked with him, "If we sleep among the books, we will soak up some knowledge." For the first time, my life had a rhythm determined by a regular work schedule instead of the chaos of hunger. I enjoyed the simplicity of each morning. I swept the floors, washed the cups, and cleaned the toilets. Then I re-shelved, dusted — and sometimes became distracted by the books. If I lost track of time, Sunee came for me and we sipped a cup of tea and ate a bowl of *jok* (rice porridge) while our son napped in the hammock. Often we did this without uttering a word, smiling shyly at each other. A small watermelon grew under Sunee's yellow sarong. I thought maybe it would be a daughter.

Three times a week, after breakfast, I headed to the nearby slums where I collected children and lead them back to the Angel Center. Although the pecking chickens seemed to know I would never harass them, they abandoned their prized worms and fled at the sound of my sandals. It amazed me how animals and people alike were conditioned by fear.

I crisscrossed the shacks, humming loud enough to be heard but lower than the racket of barking dogs. Children popped out from doors made of sarongs. The walls of the shacks were made of scrap metal. Sometimes the children simply appeared behind me. Little ones, with hair like rooster crowns, rubbed their bare stomachs, spreading dirt and sand. Tall ones with owlish eyes waited for a parent's nod giving them permission to go. The slowest ones, I thought, could not shake off the nightmares born of hunger. Shy ones itched to be enchanted by the storybooks that distracted them from the ugliness of their lives. In bare feet, they pattered beside me to the Angel Center. Herding sleepy children required patience. I enjoyed it.

They smiled while I wiped the dust from their sleepy eyes. I taught them how to wash their hands before they sat cross-legged beneath the Angel Center. From afar, they might have been healthy kids tumbling over each other in play. Up close, I saw rashes caused by insect bites. They gave their smiles freely, but their eyes told of pain. Many squirmed. Dirt reappeared on their faces soon after I wiped them. Filth was part of slum children's attire.

Even the very young sat and waited for me in the morning. They knew I would lead them to the Angel Center, where their hollow bellies were filled with a sweet coconut drink and rice. Sometimes a surprise awaited them in their drink — bits of chicken tied in a banana leaf. More energetic after eating, they stumbled like newborn animals. They grasped at legs, hands, and any other body parts within reach. Giggles filled the air. Food brought them a joy I understood.

The sight of carefree, fed children teasing each other kept me going. Unburdened by hunger, they remembered how to play and have fun. They cheered for me to take them upstairs for the next story in the picture book. Their heads filled with images and happy stories. They needed this break from their daily struggles, almost as much as food. I suspected Father Bonningue had chosen university students to volunteer for story-telling to inspire the little ones. I, too, admired these students. Once in a while, I lingered a few moments to listen to their pronunciation. This library, the only room at the Angel Center, had become the heart of my life: where I worked, where I studied, and where my family lived.

On Sundays, the routine focused on the adults in the area. Father Bonningue sang a Latin Mass in the open area under the Angel Center. Villagers crammed in, always leaving a little distance between themselves and Father Bonningue. Mass always commenced at 5:00 a.m., which allowed time for the congregants to return home and make merit to the monks collecting their morning alms.

Father Bonningue had help on that day of prayer from Dr. Jakelit, a Thai medical doctor in his thirties. With grace he handled the Bible during Mass, holding it up while Father Bonningue read. I had noticed that the doctor stood a little closer to the villagers than to Father Bonningue.

How intelligent he must have been. His parents sent him to China to study medicine at a Jesuit university. Wondering how far he traveled, I asked my friends in the library for help. The encyclopedia showed China to be northwest of Thailand. China must have been 10 to 15 times the size of my country. How did Dr. Jakelit and Father Bonningue meet in such a big place?

It pleased me that Dr. Jakelit and I shared a similar build and appearance. We could have been brothers born 12 years apart. But education in Thailand sharply divided the haves and have-nots into separate universes. While Father Bonningue and Dr. Jakelit could have never passed as siblings, their faith connected them.

***

In a corner of the library, I closed the book on the essay I had been reading and leaned back in my favorite chair. There, at the hottest part of the day, everything was still. Even the cicadas appeared to be napping. The library was all mine. I relished this time with the books. I did my best thinking there.

Because I was guided by knowledge, the ancestral ghosts remained at bay. In those six months, my head seemed overcrowded with the teachings of the Buddha, God, and Jesus. Sometimes my thoughts swirled like a tropical rainstorm. I wished my mother was there. Did she believe all the teachings of the Buddha? Did she believe we were born into such poverty, or that father died early because we did something wrong in a previous life? Did she ever hear of God and Jesus? I struggled to accept a religion that accepted foreigners and Thai people.

I read some of the Jesuit writings. This idea of God confused me. He held the position of father, shepherding his followers, commanding their obedience. But He also held the power to grant redemption to the fallen, if you asked Him for forgiveness and repented. He may absolve you of your sins so you could avoid hell. Could this God save me? After everything I had done? Could this God love me enough to save me from a disastrous reincarnation?

When I first came to the Angel Center, I wanted to master the English language and read books. Maybe I should have stayed away from the religious works translated into Thai by the Jesuits. Once I started, I craved more. The biblical text told of Mary, the mother of Jesus. I searched for the hidden message in the same way children looked for the meaning in a folktale. I kept reading to find answers to mysteries such as the virgin birth. Thinking about Mary's story made my mind spin like a top. Three years ago, I was thirsty for knowledge. Later on, I had too many questions. And I was hungry for answers.

Father Bonningue never talked to me about God. However I discovered the books that did. Reading them transported me to a world of compassion and forgiveness determined by God's will. When I felt lonely, I read the Bible to learn more about this Christian faith.

Father Bonningue believed God was in everything. The Jesuits, his brothers, said that before God there was nothing. Then God created everything. Everything. He was the originator of all things: the stars, the moon, the sky, the grass, the ocean, the fish, and the people. The "will of God" determined all. I began reading the Old Testament, which recounted the origin of the world. I had never thought about this before. At the temple, we were told there was no beginning or ending. I found it complicated. And I was too concerned about achieving the next level of study to ask. Still, I wondered, who created God?

I preferred the passages about the flood, and Abraham, and the march to Egypt. The writing weaved characters and events in the same grand way as the legends in our *Jatakas*. But my mind kept returning to the concept of God. The idea that I might have been created by Him troubled me. Why would He create me in this way, with this hard life? Was it God's will that I was born in a small village? Did something interfere with God's plans so my parents died, and I lived the life of an orphan? Why would God want me to have the life I have had? Could something overpower God's plans?

I thought of what my mother had taught me. They were the Buddha's teaching because we are Thai. We have to be good to be born human. A parrot must live in harmony with nature, not taking more than it needs. With good *karma*, it was reborn into human form. We suffered because we did something bad in our former life. We had to correct it and accept it. Until then, suffering would permeate our life. I kept coming back to one question: What awful thing did I do in my previous life? If I didn't know what it was, how could I redress it? I got up and paced. What about my next life? It would be worse than this one. What if I had to pay for what I did in the jungle? Why did the Buddha teach enlightenment, but our belief system offered no means for obtaining salvation? Then it occurred to me. What if … my legs weakened. I dropped to the floor, brought my knees to my chest, and wrapped my arms round them. No. It was impossible. No! I could not have done the same in the last life. What if—? I shook my head. No, I refused to believe it.

Trembling with sweat pouring down my face, I forced myself to follow the logic. I had to go where it led me. Maybe I survived the jungle because I had acquired the skills in my previous life. But I lost control and ended up in the same place, with dirty hands. That would have explained why I lost my parents. Maybe they died young because of me, to punish me. Could my *karma* have been so polluted? And then … I had come full circle. What would it cost me in the next life?

The screams from the jungle and the horrors of those days mixed with images of my innocent babies. Wracked with convulsions I collapsed, shivering, onto the floor. Neither the Buddha's teachings nor the robes had prepared me to sacrifice my children. I would torch every temple before allowing my children to pay for my past offenses.

CHAPTER SIXTEEN

"*KHUN* AMPORN, I wish for you to represent the Angel Center at a regional conference in Bangkok."

"What does this mean, Father Bonningue? What will I have to do? I lack qualifications and social standing. How will I know what to say? They will reject me at once."

Father Bonningue raised his hand as he did before the morning Mass.

"*Khun* Amporn, you have worked here for three years. You have supervised the interns from Tsammasart University, who are completing their programs in social welfare. You have studied at the university of life."

What a ridiculous idea. I needed a degree to be respected in my country. Some say the poor could change their lives if they were strongly motivated. Some think hollow stomachs mean hollow brains. What nonsense. If a hungry child never learns to read and write, how could he or she change their life? I turned off the voice in my head and listened to Father Bonningue.

"You understand how the poor people in Thailand survive. You understand what it is to live without money, respect, and hope. You could make a valuable contribution to the success of the conference."

I smiled broadly. My ego wanted to go … but I thought I had to turn it down. I was unworthy of this honor but Father Bonningue kept talking.

"The Jesuits organized this month-long conference to focus on the 'Social Economics Life of Asia.' You will be expected to attend meetings every day. You have met some of the priests who will be there. I expect you to help me prepare the agenda. We must convince the attendees of Thailand's unique conditions. Too many Europeans think Thailand is the same as Indochina. We both know their histories have led to dramatically different, socio-political, and economic outcomes."

My breathing accelerated. I implored his God: I hoped that he would move on to another topic. I did not want to talk of the Indochina War.

"We need to make them understand the differences. Do you think you can help with the preparation, maintain your work at the Angel Center, and attend the conference?"

"Yes! *Kap*. Yes."

My voice bounced off the crammed shelves and floated through the open window. I imagined it landing in the hammock where Sunee coddled our infant son, Ampol. Another boy, our third child.

***

Preparing for the conference, I felt energized. While we sorted and stacked documents, Father Bonningue lectured me on why the poor suffered injustices. His views on oppression sometimes confounded me. He made it sound as if a choice existed. However, his reasons differed from those of the university students. He thought the problem rested on the poor's inaccessibility to education, not their lack of effort. He advocated change through empowerment. He believed groups could unite into collectives and help each other out of poverty. But first came food and shelter, then education.

God's word may have nourished depleted souls with hope, but Father Bonningue's offered practical solutions. The idea of rearranging things to accommodate my dreams still seemed grandiose to me.

We were taking a break from sorting the conference documents on the library table.

I said, "Father Bonningue, why do *farangs* have a God who shows them forgiveness and kindness? Are they more fair-minded? If so, maybe we Thai people need to find God too?"

He burst into one of his hearty laughs. "*Khun* Amporn, God holds no passport. He comes for all men. God accepts everyone who believes, regardless of their nationality, skin color, or how much money they have. You simply have to believe in your heart."

"Like Dr. Jakelit has done? He was reincarnated into a good life. He has good *karma*. Any god would be happy to call him son."

"*Khun* Amporn, God loves you in the same way he loves Dr. Jakelit."

I felt angry. Father Bonningue wanted me to believe in folktales. I lowered my head, ashamed of my disrespect. Bad *karma* kept me from belonging to a family. Things I did to survive prevented me from being accepted. I was a loser, an outcast.

"Father, I have made too many mistakes. You call them 'sins.' I have big sins in my past."

"That is why God sent us His son Jesus, to show His love — for all of us. He also offers us redemption. We simply have to ask for His forgiveness."

God may forgive us, I thought, but what about others? Regardless of their outward politeness or good intentions, regular people would never welcome me. I was worried. Suppose the only reason the symposium participants treated me with respect was because I was with Father Bonningue. If God had such power, why did His followers need to come together to understand the importance of social justice?

***

After the conference ended, I spent more time reading the Bible. And I began to believe in this God who had the power to save people from hell. He had accepted thieves into His Kingdom.

My family and I stood together, straight as a bamboo fence. I was the tallest bamboo and the most at ease. I knew deep within me that we were doing the right thing.

I gazed at Sunee, always at my side, and our three children: Piak, my eldest son at 3 years old, so serious; Toum, my only daughter, smiled, held her brother's hand and wiggled her fat little baby legs back and forth. In Sunee's arms, 2 month old Ampol ("Noum") cooed and played with his toes. The children were too young to comprehend the enormity of that moment. This marked a turning point for all of us. I was 27, a husband and a father. They would grow up with a different belief than I had.

Father Joli stood at the front of his church, the Church of Fatima. In the pews, a few fervent parishioners witnessed the baptism of the Wathanavongs family. Dr. Jakelit stood tall among them. He had accepted to be our godfather. His kindness to my family created a debt too large to ever repay.

"*Khun* Amporn, do you accept to be a child of God and accept to place your fate in the hands of God who sent His son, Jesus Christ, to redeem us of our sins?"

The longing to belong and have a family, which had burdened me since childhood, had vanished. Loneliness had become my foe. Joy, hope and possibility had replaced it.

"I do," I said, submitting to God's will for me.

Father Joli said, "*Khun* Sunee, do you accept to be a child of God and accept to place your fate in the hands of God who sent His son, Jesus Christ, to redeem us of our sins?"

Sunee looked at me for approval. I nodded to her.

"I do," she said.

Father Joli spoke.

"*Khun* Amporn and Sunee, parents of Theerachai, Mathia, and Ampol, do you wish your children to be accepted into the family of God?"

"Yes, we do," we answered in unison.

"*Khun* Amporn and Sunee, do you agree to raise your children in the Catholic faith until they become old enough to confirm their wish to be part of God's family?"

"Yes, we do."

"Welcome into God's family."

Father Joli poured a drop of blessed water on each of our foreheads and traced a cross. Noum giggled when Father Joli touched his forehead. Piak reached for his baby sister's hand.

Father Joli led us to a spot in front of the altar.

"*Khun* Amporn and *Khun* Sunee, as members of the Church of Fatima and as children of God, I wish to bless your union. What God unites cannot be parted by man."

To me, he said, "You must promise to love, to protect, and to support *Khun* Sunee."

Then to her, he said, "*Khun* Sunee, you must promise to honor and respect *Khun* Amporn."

Father Joli reached for our left hands and showed us how to intertwine our fingers. He held our united hands between his.

"*Khun* Amporn, do you accept *Khun* Sunee as your wife?"

"I do."

"*Khun* Sunee, do you accept *Khun* Amporn as your husband?"

"I do."

Father Joli looked up. "In the name of God, I unite Amporn and Sunee, as husband and wife in the unity of the Holy Spirit. In the powers vested in me, I declare you husband and wife."

I looked at my wife. We belonged to one another before God. My family belonged to God's family. My children would never be orphans.

***

"What do you think? Does it interest you?"

Here we go again. Father Bonningue and I were in the library behind closed doors.

"Please explain it to me again. Slowly." I asked.

"*Khun* Amporn, such rare opportunities rarely arise. You cannot say '*non*'."

The French "no" hung between us. He wanted me to put a "yes" in its place. I felt pulled in different directions. I had a family to think of. I enjoyed my life as it was then. Still, my colorful feathers strained to be seen. Since leaving my Buddhist studies, my peacock plumage had had few opportunities for display.

"I have been contacted by one of the colleges of Xavier University. It is in the Philippines. They offer one year scholarships to Asian students to train them for social leadership roles in their communities. The school will pay for classes, housing, and transportation, plus a weekly allowance for food."

"Tell me more about the school."

"SEARSOLIN stands for the South East Asian Rural Social Leadership Institute. I can recommend you very highly, especially after all your work at the Angel Center and the Jesuit Conference last year. You are an ideal candidate. Think of it. At the end of the year, you would be fluent in English. All the courses are taught in English."

My imagination was a wild tiger leaping at the opportunity. After the year at Xavier, I knew I would be an educated man. I saw myself in a black suit, white shirt, light blue tie, and laced black shoes. Mornings, before leaving our two-room house for work, I planted a light kiss on Sunee's forehead and waved to little Piak. I did not need a nail for my straw hat, only a shelf for my briefcase. I breathed in this new image of myself. It smelled sweet.

Another image crowded in. Sunee and the children, crying, when they waved good-bye to me for a year. One full year apart. Could we manage? Was this a ghost in disguise, waiting to trip me up? A dark cloud covered the sun. Would I lose my job at the Angel Center? How far was it to the Philippines? Would I be able to follow classes in English? How would I make money if I had to study all day? Could Sunee manage by herself?

I examined the books on the shelves. I knew all of them personally. With my years in the temples, they formed the universe of my learning. The geography of my life had been bordered by small villages, the jungle, Bangkok, and the Angel Center. What if a different, better life lay beyond the borders? I had a headache.

"Do you think this is God's will for me, Father Bonningue? To put my family through so much difficulty while I enjoy studying for a degree? It seems like the sin of selfishness to me."

I looked at him, praying he would validate my strong desire to go.

"Son, only you can determine if He calls upon you to serve in this way. Our path can be inconvenient at times. Serving Him led me to Asia. I prefer cheese and French baguettes to rice and curry. But that was not His will for me." Patting his belly, he laughed.

"I need to think about this. May I have a few days?" I glanced out the library window at the spring sky.

"Of course, *Khun* Amporn."

CHAPTER SEVENTEEN

I WALKED down the airplane aisle looking for seat 25A. People, mostly men, mostly foreigners, placed bags and suitcases in the storage area above the seats. I had nothing to stow. My passport was tucked in my shirt pocket. Night had fallen, some passengers were already nodding off in their seats, but I was wide-awake. I was anxious to embark on this new chapter of my life, which was to begin in three short hours.

"Flight 015 from Bangkok to Manila has completed boarding. In preparation for takeoff, please stow your belongings, bring the back of your chair to an upright position, and securely fasten your seat belt. The captain has turned on the no-smoking sign. Once we have reached our cruising altitude, the captain will update us on our course and time of arrival. Please sit back, relax, and enjoy your flight. Thank you for flying with KLM Royal Dutch Airlines today."

Outside the plane window, everything moved with purpose. Suitcases rolled up a ramp and then dropped into the plane's gut. Men with odd-looking ear covers buzzed around. Somehow they avoided bumping into each other. Carts, hoses, and pieces of machinery fed the plane. My stomach somersaulted.

The large, steel blades picked up speed, spinning faster. Soon the airplane trembled. I covered my ears against the deafening noise, which reminded me of the rat-tat-tat of artillery. The noise brought on nausea. I shoved the memories back where they belonged, deep inside.

When the plane lifted off the ground, I settled down and watched the signs and lights become white dots, candle flames in a dark temple. The moon reflected on the ocean.

"*Sowai*, beautiful," I whispered to Sunee. Of course she could not hear me, but it made me feel closer to her. The approaching clouds swallowed the plane. Then I addressed my mother.

"Mommy, I wish you could see this. I am flying through the skies to a new life. It is a miracle. If you believed in God, you would be up here in heaven and we would be closer to each other."

I reclined my seat, hoping to nap. While waiting to drift off, I watched a slow-motion movie of my life over the last few weeks. After Sunee agreed that I should take this opportunity, Father Bonningue told me I had been granted a scholarship for the Xavier program. God's magic had been present in that moment. Why else would that sort of thing have happened to me? For the first time, Father Bonningue had embraced me. His voice still resonated in my head: "Congratulations, *Khun* Amporn. I knew you would be accepted. You make me proud of you. God bless you."

He released me and walked away, singing in French. The once free-flowing rhythm of my life had changed. A new set of problems came with my decision to go away to school for a year. Sunee and the children could not possibly come with me. I had to sort out where they would live and how I would feed my family without a job. I wondered whether my children would think I had abandoned them. A year was such a long time in a young child's life. That thought alone terrified me more than any concerns I may have had about my ability to survive the year at school without any money.

I found answers to the problems one by one. A few kilometers from the Angel Center I found a small plot of land to rent for 25 *baht* a month. I took my entire life's savings from the cooking-oil canister and bought wood planks, plywood, and corrugated metal sheets. The father of Surasak, one of the students at the Angel Center, offered to help me build a hut. Together we worked for two days, until we had a more-or-less acceptable shelter for my family. Although it looked like an oversized wooden crate wearing a steel hat, I thought it should withstand any storm. Sunee and the three children had room to lie next to each other on a straw mattress at night. And there was space left over for sheltering a few things during the rainy season.

I spent every evening trying to scrape together more money. I cut grass again, a reminder of why I wanted a better future. When I was unable to find work, I collected newspapers for Sunee. She hung them to dry. Later, she made bags out of them and sold them at the market. Every time I dropped extra coins in the canister, I told myself that my dream would become real and my family would not starve. Sunee assured me they would have enough to eat. She grew more herbs, mint and basil, and a few extra vegetables – carrots, onions, and whatever else the tired soil next to our hut could be cajoled into producing.

At times, I thought I detected pride in her voice when she said "our home" or "our land." It made me wonder if she missed her father's home. I was sure she did not miss him. Her smile had grown more carefree and her posture more confident than when we had first met. Perhaps she wanted to show how she, too, could take care of our family. Or maybe I was convincing myself that this was a necessary step back before taking a great leap forward. Our godfather, Dr. Jakelit, helped too. He gave me four cotton shirts, one with long sleeves. "You'll need it," he said. Then he added two cotton jackets similar to the ones men wear in offices; three pairs of pants, five pairs of socks, one pair of black leather shoes, an English Bible, a few pens, three notebooks, and an old brown leather medicine bag to hold everything. I could not help but wonder how different Dr. Jakelit's send-off to Beijing to study medicine must have been. Still, I was grateful that he supported my plan.

The thought that I would earn a certificate gave me hope for a better future. My decision made sense, I told myself. I had wanted a family for so long; to leave it scared me. I had to make something out of that opportunity. I wanted to learn perfect English and have a chance at getting an office job.

A hand on my left shoulder drew me out of my reverie. I opened my eyes to the sight of a woman in a purple uniform. She held a tray.

"Sir, would you like a meal?"

I was startled that someone with a strange accent addressed me as "sir."

"Yes, please," I replied, minding my "l."

***

I was one of 17 students in the classroom. Large windows let in the bright Filipino sun. The room smelled clean. Identical desks and chairs sat in neat rows. Everyone looked serious and nervous. They had traveled from all corners of Asia to converge in my garden of dreams. Clean-cut black haircuts poked through the collars of pressed, white shirts. The young men wore trousers in shades of beige, grey, and blue. Between a few coughs, the breeze could be heard blowing through.

The founder of Xavier University, Fr. William Masterson, delivered the opening address. In the familiar-looking Jesuit robe, he reminded me of Father Bonningue. A small, empty space manifested in my stomach. I reminded myself that I no longer faced the world alone. Little Lek had matured into a responsible father. *Khun* Amporn was a scholarship recipient! At least half of my classmates were scholarship recipients. The other half came from well-heeled circumstances. They intimidated me. I lacked family connections in which to ground my hopes for success.

"Welcome, everyone, to the South East Asia Rural Social Leadership Institute. You are the founding student body of this program. You, the first class, will graduate in May 1964. We hope you will heed the call to become leaders in your rural communities when you return home. Together you represent Thailand, Malaysia, South Korea, Hong Kong, and, of course, our host country, the Philippines."

My thoughts drifted momentarily. I imagined myself speaking fluent English with a secure office job in Bangkok. I even saw myself assisting others. I squirmed in my seat. I wondered what my classmates were thinking.

"Our mission here at SEARSOLIN is to train you to become active leaders in education and agricultural development in the improvement of rural productivity through organizations which foster moral and economic development. We aspire to educate you to become strong figures within your communities. You have been chosen for your integrity, your demonstrated talent to work with people, and for your potential to work for a just social order founded on the ideals of the dignity of man. Together with the rural villagers in your country, and through the institutions you will help create when you return home, you will improve agricultural productivity, strengthening the moral, economic, and spiritual foundations of your communities."

My mind caught on the words "the dignity of man." I wondered how many of the scholarship recipients had walked with their heads low, shamed by poverty.

Moral leadership did not rise from growling stomachs, squalor, or unspeakable acts committed in the name of survival.

"Before concluding, I want to share one of my deepest convictions with you: Visions beget dreams — which so often, no matter how ridiculed, no matter how seemingly impossible from so many angles, human and financial — have ways of coming true. Go, study hard, and dream of the possibilities."

Many heads nodded. I agreed. Dreams were the purview of the poor; they did not cost anything, yet they kept you alive.

"Please enjoy your time here. The Philippines extend warm hospitality to their visitors. The country has entered a period of economic development. Discover our host city, Cagayan de Oro. It is a melting pot of Filipino culture. You will love the sweetness of their pineapples. You may prefer them to those of your country. Even if you do not, you will think differently after you have tried these, if you keep an open mind."

We smiled in unison, dispelling the tension in the room.

"Take time during your studies to meet one another, exchange ideas, and learn outside the classroom. I also recommend visiting the St. Augustine Metropolitan Cathedral. You will find the architecture magnificent and our archbishop most eloquent. He firmly supports our efforts here at the university."

Father Bonningue had recommended my visiting the cathedral, which he found "*incroyable*." I had learned the English translation to mean "incredible." I wanted to see this cathedral. I did not want to disappoint Father Bonningue.

"Welcome, again. If any of you need assistance, please make an appointment to meet with me. We want you to be comfortable so you can focus on learning. May God bless you all."

***

"Come in, Mr. Wa-ta-vnong." Father Masterson slowed his pronunciation of my name but still managed to discard a few letters. He spoke in a strange accent, which I had yet to decipher. I assumed it was American but had no idea. As I stood before him, my head reached his shoulder. I had never set eyes on such a tall man. Yet his kindness towered over his height. He was warm like Father Bonningue. Everything about this giant servant of God — his gaze, features, and handshake — put me at ease.

He smiled and offered me a seat on the brown couch. Behind it, a low table held a few books and pamphlets. Father Masterson sat in a high-backed, red, leather chair with worn armrests. His chin rested on his chest. He looked at me over black-rimmed glasses and stroked his chin. He had a half-moon of white hair and a shiny head. He observed me with intent, as if wanting to figure me out. Others said he was always busy. He showed no sign of being in a hurry.

"Thank you for making an appointment to see me. So few students believe my offer to be sincere. I enjoy meeting with students. And the success of this new program is very close to my heart. Rural people all over the region need strong leaders. But people must first be educated if they are to rise to the challenge." Father Masterson paused. His smile broadened. He waved his hand in the air while he spoke. I thought Father Bonningue had said it was a French habit.

"You have to excuse me. Sometimes my enthusiasm for the program converts me into a preacher. I believe strongly that the graduates can make a difference. How do you enjoy your classes?"

A large desk with a red leather blotter dominated the room. His chair could have held two of me. The frame was carved with intricate patterns. I wondered what angels did such fine work. Leather-bound books, some with golden lettering, lined the walls. Certificates in Latin and Italian hung on the walls. The room was grand. Even the feather pen resting in the ink bottle appeared noble. I took in every detail. I wanted to remember the beauty of the most refined place I had ever set foot in.

"Mr. Wa-ta-nog, do you speak English?" Father Masterson asked.

"Yes. Yes."

I lowered my eyes before continuing. "The program is very good. I will benefit greatly. Thailand suffers from much poverty. We have good land for fruits, rice, and wood, but lack know-how. Thai people appreciate what they have. They smile a lot. They help each other. I enjoy studying, so I will work hard to speak English very good. Um, I mean very well."

"Yes, yes," Father Masterson said. "Now, what can I help you with?"

"Father Bonningue, at the Angel Center in Bangkok where I worked, gave my job to another man when I left. He needs help every day. He could not manage a year without assistance. I have a family back home, a wife and three children. We were baptized by Father Joli at the Church of Fatima."

"Yes, yes, go on." He glanced at the mountain of papers on his desk.

"With my scholarship, I get 450 *pesos* every month for myself. I can manage without this money. My family in Thailand, they need the money very bad. Could the money go to them? It would be enough for my wife and my children to live while I apply myself here."

I took a deep breath and stared at my hand-me-down shoes. I had lowered myself to begging again. Would my life ever change?

"Before I left, my wife started selling paper bags at the market to earn money. But they do not sell well. She grows vegetables and sells some at the market. We have a small plot of land, too small to feed the family but enough to grow a few extra herbs to sell." I thought about Sunee.

"Father, my wife is brave, but courage does not feed empty stomachs."

"This could set a precedent if we were to send money to your family."

"Father Masterson, my country is poorer than the Philippines. My family takes a big risk accepting for me to come here for one year. My parents died young, leaving me orphaned. I understand what it takes to survive. I have a plan. I …"

Father Masterson raised his hands, in the same manner Father Bonningue did before singing Mass to indicate silence. I stopped in mid-sentence, afraid to look up. Frozen with fear, I was sure he would throw me out of his office or send me home in shame.

"Oh? We want you to focus on your studies and return home with new knowledge and skills. How can you work and achieve this?" Father Masterson glanced at the standing clock ticking in the corner.

"Father Masterson, I am a good student. I love books above anything. I promise you, my studies will be my priority." I refrained from explaining how I developed strict self-discipline during my years as a monk. I wanted him to trust my Catholic devotion.

"You see, Father Masterson, excellent memory was God's special gift to me. I can study very good and—"

"You can study very well," Father Masterson said. "Tell me your plan."

"It is simple. You send the money to my family through Father Bonningue so they can eat and pay the rent. Then I not have to worry about them. I will be able to concentrate on my studies with all my attention." I paused, seeking approval.

With a wave of his hand, he told me to continue.

"I will find a way to make enough money from odd jobs here. I have experience cutting grass, cooking, taking care of children, organizing documents, and using a hammer. I am confident I will find work that will fit in with our class schedule. Please give me your permission. I promise to be a good student." I grinned, hoping the Thai smile would work its magic.

"We overlooked the possibility of this being a problem for our students. Your classmates, they continue to receive their salary while studying here. Why does your situation differ?"

"The Angel Center is very small. Father Bonningue has created a large community. He requires assistance to fulfill his commitments. Many children live in great need in the slums of Bangkok where the Center operates. When I left, he had to hire someone else. My being here is a great sacrifice for my family. I am afraid for Sunee. A mother will—" I stopped myself just in time. I was going to say, "… do anything, even steal to feed her children." What would Father Masterson have thought of us? I lowered my gaze.

He brought his hands together in prayer, and lowered his head. I pressed my sweaty palms into my trousers. My left leg shook. I wanted my future and my family's well-being to be in my hands. I refused to beg anymore. He had to say yes.

He took a deep breath.

I waited for the verdict.

"You seem to be a very serious man, Mr. Wa-ta-nog. I will agree to your proposal. However, I will be asking your teachers about your progress. This new program must succeed if we wish to create others. We do not want people coming to SEARSOLIN because they think they can make money from a second job while receiving a stipend. Yet, when we see a student willing to work diligently to find solutions for their economic hardships, we have found the right people for our program. If you can find solutions for yourself and your family, maybe you have the talent to lead your villagers to solutions at home."

I exhaled.

"Thank you, Father Masterson. My family and I appreciate your kind support and consideration. I will make you proud of my results." I performed a traditional *wei* with a deep bow.

I noticed the large bronze cross above the door and nodded to it.

"Thank you, God," I whispered as I left.

CHAPTER EIGHTEEN

MY FIRST week at SEARSOLIN rushed by like a tropical wind. The classes fascinated me. I learned how agriculture serves as the undercurrent of our economy, how our farms are organized and our agronomic structure leads to the dire situation of families at the Angel Center, not the vagaries of Mother Nature. Poverty is easier to reverse than I had ever imagined. The power of a group captivated me. By pooling resources and knowledge and spreading risk among many, a community could alter the cycle of devastation when an ox died or a drought occurred.

While learning and searching for solutions excited me, sometimes my personal situation intruded into my happy hours in the classroom. Thoughts of Sunee struggling to feed our family distracted me. I saw little Mathia rubbing her stomach while Piak tried to amuse her and divert her attention. My conscience gnawed at me worse than vermin. My meager savings dwindled with each passing day. What I was learning was too important to abandon. Still, my conscience weighed in: Is this more important than your children's needs? I ignored it.

***

Sunday arrived — the first day without classes. The morning air carried excitement. My classmates were about to leave on an adventure. Familiar with impoverishment but unaccustomed to the discipline of long hours in class, they could not wait to unleash their pent-up energy in Cagayan de Oro. Like street kids everywhere, they were deciding whether to fill up their bellies or play. Their voices rose as they jostled each other and abandoned their Jesuit-inspired studious airs. I hung back.

"Lord's day of rest, no studying today," one said.

"I have a stomach upset," I said. "You go ahead, and I'll join you next week."

I grimaced and held my belly for effect.

The teasing aromas of fried squid balls, barbecued pork, and my favorite Filipino treat, *macapuno*, a mix of coconut meat, tapioca, and jelly topped with ice cream, would make me hungrier. I knew I must not squander my last few dollars on food. A dark mood overtook me. The ebb and flow of working at the Angel Center had lulled me into forgetting I was still a debtor in this life. I could not even afford street food. Sourness traveled from my stomach to my mouth. Feeling weary, I retreated to my dorm room.

***

"James, what are you doing here? Aren't you going to town with the others?" I asked my roommate. It surprised me to find him reading on his bed.

"I am tired. It's been a lot of changes this week. Besides, my mom makes the best Filipino food. I'll wait to visit the town another time." He returned to his book.

Awkward over the newness of our situation, we danced around one another, nodding politely and half-smiling when our eyes met.

After an hour or so, James broke the stillness.

"Amporn, you dislike exploring the city?"

"No, but I need time to think. I worry about my family. I left them with all my money. I don't have enough to make it through the year. Father Masterson agreed to send them my stipend. I must earn something soon, or I will starve long before we graduate. I had to leave my job in Bangkok. I …" I stopped in mid-sentence. My thoughts escaped uncensored. My face burned from the shameful outburst. I looked at James, wondering how he would react.

He dropped his book, moved to the side of the bed, and shook his head.

"I understand. I feel troubled too. If I fail my studies, it will be a disgrace for my family, and bring us financial ruin." James took off his wire-rimmed glasses and cleaned them with a corner of his collarless white shirt. With his glasses back on his nose, he straightened his shirt and sighed, filling the space between us with his own sorrows.

James Gomez was the son of a carpenter. Judging by the roughness of his hands, I guessed he had spent more time working than studying. His hands said he had reached his sixties. Yet he was my age, 27. He tiptoed around campus, a scared rabbit searching for a place to burrow while the other students searched with enthusiasm for a new way of life.

I thought James, as a Filipino, had more pressure on him than the rest of us. Failure had far broader implications for him. Success was expected, and not just by his family. SEARSOLIN wanted a local role model to showcase; a graduate who would emerge from this program as a force of social change in the local community; a tribute to the Jesuits and their philosophy.

I wondered if James chose to come here or if some greater force swept him onto the campus. If he succeeded, he would change the course of his entire family's fortune. It would be as if he and his family had tapped into some unknown groundwater and suddenly farmed delicious marketable fruit trees, which blossomed into a full orchard. It would be the kind of success that would last for generations! If he failed, I did not want to think about what that would mean for all of them.

I sat on the edge of my bed, facing James.

"I understand. I had to quit my job. No work waits for me at home. I must graduate with skills to improve my chances in Bangkok. I owe it to my family — they have suffered hardship because of my absence. But surviving this year comes first."

The silence sucked my dwindling optimism. I knew how this worked. Sheltered under a market stall, you resented the falling rain, and were grateful to be dry. Then the wood-soaked table began to drip. The wetness reached your bones and you stopped wanting to find a dry spot. Soaking wet, you wondered, "What's the point?" Your spirits defeated you before the rain ever did.

I paced back and forth. It helped me to sort out my thoughts.

I said, "No one will hire me off-campus if they know I study here. They want to avoid trouble with the Jesuits. I thought about polishing shoes. Then I realized most students have only one pair."

I stared at James, challenging him to get out of the rain before he got too wet.

"I used to cut grass in Bangkok for extra money," I told him. "Maybe I could work in the campus gardens. What do you think?"

James looked surprised. Perhaps it was because I sought his opinion. Or maybe he found my idea ridiculous. He came out of his shell.

"I don't think it would work, Amporn. Jesuit brothers tend to the gardens every Saturday. Have you been so absorbed in your studies you didn't notice? For them, gardening is a labor of love. I think it is also an opportunity to work outdoors, away from the students."

I felt relieved at letting the monkey out of my head. It was good to talk to someone with a similar background. Intimacy, something very new to me, bound us. For the first time, I experienced a sense of community with another man who was my peer. Each of us battled to cut the strings controlled by the ghosts of our ancestors. We were not squabbling over the morsels society threw to the less fortunate. We were struggling to create a place for ourselves within society. What if together we found a better way? We had to expose our struggles and find solutions. Why live in embarrassment that kept us isolated and weak?

"I need to find something our classmates require. Something I can do for them that costs less than they now pay for the service. What do you think, James? Help me."

He looked shocked. "You would work for our classmates? You want them to realize you are poverty-stricken? Then they would guess why you never join them in town. Do you think they would still respect you? I hate nothing more than being treated as poor by poor people."

James' shoulders slouched lower than I thought possible. He looked away from me and stared at the wall. I thought I had lost him to his demons.

"Poverty ruled my life at an early age," I told him. "In the village market where I grew up in Thailand, no one respected me. So I learned to ignore them. I will make something of myself this year. If I can learn English very good, uh, very well, I will get an office job with a title. Then, everybody will respect me."

James remained unconvinced.

"What do you find the hardest here?" I asked.

"Learning. A lot of what they teach us confuses me. How can I remember what makes no sense to me? I worry all the time about examinations. If I fail …"

I had seen the look in his eyes — the shadow of resignation accompanying surrender. He was too young. I wanted him to defy the odds, to stand up to life and demand better. I refused to be pushed around any longer because we were born destitute.

"James, how much do they charge in town to launder and press a pair of trousers and a shirt?"

He glanced at me with an expression of confusion. He peered over the top of his glasses, a habit when he was deep in thought.

"Yes, quite expensive. They charge 3 *pesos* per shirt and the same for a pair of trousers."

"We found a solution!" Hope filled me. I jumped to my feet and pulled a pair of black socks from my drawer. Fishing inside for my remaining savings, I counted $8 U.S. James' eyebrows shot up.

"You found a solution?" he said.

"And an iron costs how much?" I asked.

"Five U.S. dollars," he said. "I wanted to buy one so I could press my own clothes, but who has that kind of money?" His forehead creased into a frown.

"Exactly why this will work!"

Energy took the place of my gloom. I shoved the dollars back into my sock and tossed it to James like a hot potato. He threw it back at me.

"What if I offered to wash and press shirts and trousers for 2 *pesos* each? Our classmates would save 2 *pesos* per cleaning. They would avoid an extra trip to town and could use their savings for weekend outings. I would pick up the clothes from their rooms and deliver their clean laundry, pressed and folded."

Pacing from one end of our box-size room to the other, I calculated the number of students, the time it would take, and how much I could make per week. My pace picked up. I saw a way out of my predicament. But I needed James' cooperation. Without it, the plan would fall apart. One complaint about the drying shirts or the heat of the steam iron to Father Masterson would derail the plan. Most of all, it was essential to keep our classmates from embarrassing James.

"James, would you mind if I did this on Saturdays and Sundays when our roommates leave for the day? Your studies come first, so I will be very quiet. I can answer questions while I iron. I'll use the common bathroom to wash the clothes early in the morning, before the others are up. The clothes can dry here in our room. I will iron and fold before our classmates return from their Sunday outings."

He did not look happy. I wondered what bothered him. I shuffled back and forth and continued to calculate. *Let's say, 4 pesos times eight which is half the students in our class. That makes 24 pesos per student four times a week. Multiply that by four weeks per month that makes 96 pesos.* James interrupted.

"You mean you will be a servant to our classmates?"

The question hung between us. I hesitated with my response. James suffered more than I from his low-class status. I accepted my position years ago and then promised myself to control my life's outcome. How I reached my goals did not matter. In 12 months, I would leave this country. I would change the fortune of my family. I did not care what our classmates thought. But I had to please James. I could not risk his complaining to Father Masterson that my plan disturbed his studies.

I pulled a chair in front of James and sat, careful to keep a comfortable distance. "James, remember last week when Father Masterson welcomed us? He told us we needed to create organizations to improve productivity based on moral foundations."

"Yes, I remember," James said as he leaned back.

I held my position.

"I intend to test whether it works in real life." I gave him time to digest my words.

"You and I understand that poor people are caught in a struggle for survival. They focus on having enough food for today. They work long hours. At the end of the day, they are too tired to plan or figure out a different way, a better way. They never have time to rest, let alone relax. But if two people help each other, maybe it can turn out differently."

James looked into my eyes. "What do you mean?" he said.

"You helped me figure out this idea. Maybe you could pick up the clothes and deliver them when—"

"No! I won't be their servant," he said. The force of his reply made me recoil.

My scheme required his full cooperation. I kept talking. He had to agree if I was to succeed.

"I'm sorry, I didn't mean anything of the sort. I understand."

He got up. I reached for his arm.

"James, give me a minute, please. I will think of something. I know we can make this work."

He sat down, folded his arms across his chest, and looked away.

"I know how you can help. And no one has to know. If you hang the shirts and pants to dry, and maybe do some folding, it will be faster. Working together, I mean. While I iron, I can answer your questions and help you to memorize the lessons. God blessed me with a good memory. I used to recite long verses when I was a monk."

I stopped. *Uh-oh.* I had let the peacock out.

"You were a monk?" James looked astonished.

"It's a long story. I'll tell you another time. It is not relevant. I devised tricks to help me memorize the Buddhist chants. I can show you how to do it."

"Really?"

"Really. Please say you will support me, James. We trust each other, right? Then we must stand up for each other."

He hesitated for a good long time before speaking.

"Yes, but you must tell Father Masterson about your plan. I don't want to get into trouble. Please do not mention my involvement. My family would be ashamed if they found out. I must not shame my father. He sacrifices so much for me."

I did not understand why James' father would disapprove of his son being self-reliant. Time was too precious to think about it at the moment.

"But James, I need to tell Father Masterson our concept of pooling our efforts rather than struggling individually. I want him to see how this concept of a 'collective' works in practice. I have to let him know that I've enlisted someone else."

James looked away again. I watched him slip from me.

"James, this is not a matter of choice for me. Without a way to make money, I might as well pack my bags right now. Off-campus work will be my only other option. How will I find the time to help you cram for examinations? You have my word. I will convince Father Masterson we are trying to implement our lessons on a small scale before we attempt it at home, where people's livelihoods are at stake. We will present it to anyone that asks, as putting theory into practice. Please reconsider your views on poverty, James. We were invited here to be trained in ways to overcome it. We must roll up our sleeves and explore real-world solutions."

James looked up.

"Yes. I'll agree," he said.

We shook hands, still an awkward gesture for me. The symbolism transcended my discomfort. We had sealed our fates together.

CHAPTER NINETEEN

I UNCLIPPED 10 pairs of grey trousers from the line over my bed. The shirts were slightly damp, the perfect time to iron them. To be more comfortable, I worked in my undershirt.

"James, do you mind if I do the ironing now?"

This was simply a formality. James had been very supportive since we had launched our laundry service three months earlier. Father Masterson's blessing had been important to James.

None of our classmates mentioned our business to me. And I doubted they approached James. He stopped asking me to hide the dirty laundry, as he once did. Beyond polite greetings, we seldom socialized with our housemates. They either studied in the library or, more often, visited the town or the shops on the perimeter of campus. With salaries from their jobs back home in Malaysia and Hong Kong, and their stipend, they found plenty of distractions. The program, although demanding, still left them sufficient time to enjoy the sweet, local pineapples. Our housemates made good use of the time away from their responsibilities at home.

James and I followed a different routine. We spent most of our free time in our room. Saturday afternoons and most of Sunday, James studied and I ironed. He helped me with the folding, and I answered his questions or helped him memorize class notes. Once in a while, we chatted about our families. Rarely did we mention the future.

"No, it doesn't disturb me. I enjoy hearing the clank of the iron when you put it back on the hot plate," said James. "It reminds me of my mother."

I no longer remembered time with my mother. Only the fragrance of jasmine and the memory of her humming lullabies remained. In the jungle, I had been afraid to invoke her memory. So, little by little, the details of her face and her hands were erased. I clung to memories of her scent and the sounds she made. I saw her in my mind's eye, a golden fluttering butterfly, free and happy.

"When you finish, would you help me with our economics homework? The calculations might as well be in Chinese," James said. His voice nudged me back to my steam bath.

"Yes, of course, after I return."

He looked surprised.

"Where are you going?"

"It was a light load today. I want to finish quickly and visit the cathedral. Our classmates say it is magnificent. I cannot believe we have been here almost three months. It is time for me to light a candle for our efforts and for my family at home. Would you like to come with me?"

I reached for the iron's handle and touched the base, warm but not sizzling. I wiped the hot plate to remove any charcoal smudges. I wanted no complaints. I applied myself with focused attention to my pressing job.

"No, thank you, Amporn, I must study. If I fall further behind, I should just quit. Reading everything takes me so long."

I assisted James with his homework when I could. He put in great effort, but he was blessed with more manual talent than ability for memorizing lessons. Either he attended classes or he sat in the library or at his desk, always with a book in hand. Even at night when we went to bed, I watched him straining for the last bit of light to finish one more page. Still, for all his trouble, he retained little. I imagined it had to be frustrating. It was strange, this compassion I felt for James.

I saw myself all those years ago in the marketplace, stealing food, hiding, waiting for someone to unexpectedly drop a bag or a coin I could snatch. I was famished most of the time. My life had been an uphill battle to stay alive. James had the same struggle with words and knowledge. He waited for any part of our lessons to stick.

My mind was a sponge, soaking up everything. It kept expanding to absorb whatever they taught us. Slowly the lessons seeped into the recesses of my memory. Since I was a young novice learning *Pali*, I had learned with ease. I was grateful for this talent I discovered in the robes. It gave me courage.

"Maybe a short break would help you. You crack the books day and night without any break. Sometimes I worry you will get sick. Come with me, it will refresh you." I felt particularly light that day.

James shook his head and went back to his books while I concentrated on my task. Silence flowed naturally between us.

"James, I have ironed my last shirts for today."

I returned the iron to its hiding spot under my bed, being careful with how I stored the hot plate. The thought of accidentally setting fire to the room compelled me to double-check it before I left.

"It's still early, so I will go visit the cathedral. Last chance … Why don't you come with me?"

He looked more and more tired with every passing week. The circles under his eyes had grown larger and drooped below the rims of his glasses.

"Thank you for the kind offer, Amporn, but I have at least three chapters to read before tomorrow," said James, who sighed.

"I hope you take a rest, James."

He ignored me. I put on my dress shirt and headed out the door.

***

The cool air embraced me the moment I walked into the cathedral. The caress felt so real, I shuddered. The contrast between the beating sun and the relentless street noise, and the coolness and serenity of this sanctum calmed me. It reminded me of the Angel

Center and meeting Father Bonningue for the first time. That day, my life changed in ways I could never have imagined.

I walked down the aisle into a sliver of sunlight streaming through the stained-glass window. The white ceilings seemed to reach to heaven. The natural-colored wooden beams arched above me, a protective cage drawing me to the very center of what looked like a majestic womb. The golden altar rested on rich, red carpeting. Beyond, lifelike sculpted figures of Joseph, Jesus, and Mary beckoned. I walked toward the figures in a daze.

I directed my gaze to the Virgin Mary. Though I had become unaware of my surroundings, I was fully conscious of her presence. I had seen so many pictures of her in the books at the Angel Center, but she had never been as real to me as in that moment. She stood near me, her arms crossed, her head covered in a white shawl draping over her sky-blue dress. Her soft, gentle face smiled at me.

When I reached the first pew, I dropped onto my right knee, crossed myself with my good hand, and sat down. Tears filled my eyes. I lost sight of the altar. The red carpet became a pool of blood at the feet of the Virgin.

"No!" I screamed, holding my head, pain ripping through my body. The jungle closed in on me. I was catapulted into the center of hell. My desire for deliverance overpowered the shame of my dark secret.

"Mary, Holy Virgin, Mother of God, forgive me, for I have sinned."

I knew in that moment that I needed to confess all my sins, each and every one. I wanted to bare my soul to her. She needed to understand all that I had done before I became a believer. If she could hear me out and find compassion for me, then perhaps I could finally be free of my past — the nightmares, the shame, and the loneliness. Maybe she would help me to forgive myself.

I took a deep breath. To find my courage to speak the unspeakable in this place of grace and in her presence, I started to recite, "Hail Mary, full of grace, the Lord is with thee; blessed art thou among women, and blessed is the fruit of thy womb, Jesus. Holy Mary, Mother of God, pray for us sinners, now and at the hour of our death. Amen."

With my hands held in prayer, I looked up at her. Without lowering my eyes, I began, "Blessed Mother, Mother of Jesus, please hear me, hear my sins and forgive me."

For the next three hours I spoke to her. I spared her no details. I did not blame the death of my parents for my loneliness nor my ignorance. I recounted every memory I had of stealing in the markets of Surin, whether it was a rotten mango or a few *baht* from a merchant too old to chase me. I told her how one night I had beaten one of the mongrel dogs until it bled because it reminded me too much of myself. I wept at the memory of the bleeding dog.

When my tears slowed, I could no longer shun my actions in the jungle. "Blessed Mother, remember, I was once a son too. I am in need of forgiveness for the sins I am about to confess, for they are unforgivable. Only you in your compassion and infinite wisdom can forgive me for what I have done in the jungle."

With a sudden calmness, I began to tell her about the atrocities I had perpetrated against boys and men whom I did not know. The familiar taste of hatred and self-loathing rose in my throat. It is a vile sourness that cannot be spitted out. I swallowed hard and recounted slowly every detail I could remember so as not to spare myself any shame. If she were to forgive me, she had to know everything.

When I finished, I dropped my head into my hands as I kneeled before her. Again, tears welled up. But I knew I was not done. I had one last confession to make. I looked up at her again.

"Mother Mary, You who birthed Jesus Christ, You who have given life, please forgive me, for I tried to take my own life. Not once but twice. I tried to throw away the only gift I ever possessed, my life."

The calmness that had accompanied my confession spilled out of me. A need, so sharp, and excruciating, greater than all the pain of hunger that I had ever experienced in my life, sprung from within with such urgency that I shouted out, "Please forgive me, Mother Mary. I have sinned and ask for your forgiveness. Only you can offer me redemption."

Spent, I hoisted myself onto the pew. I stared at her. And in the silence that embraced us, I knew she had forgiven me. She could see Lek, Boney, and Amporn. She saw all of me. She knew everything. I had spared her nothing.

"Mother Mary."

The words tumbled out of my consciousness before I spoke them. "Mother, Virgin Mary, Mother of all of God's children. My Mother," I whispered.

Through the window, a sliver of light shone on her face. Warmth seeped into the empty space lodged in my soul since my mother's death. I sat quietly until the hollowness vanished.

"Thank you for your forgiveness," I whispered to her. I was now a son again.

I walked out of the cathedral into the Filipino streets. The setting sun glimmered. Children were playing on front stoops under the watchful eyes of their mothers.

CHAPTER TWENTY

JAMES BEGAN teasing me after my visit to the cathedral. He said I returned a changed man.

"I wonder, Amporn, what kind of temple you visited. Was it the type with a strong female presence?"

He smiled and kissed the air.

"Stop. Why do you say such things? You know I am married and loyal to my wife. I would never dishonor her. Besides, I have no such desires."

James sighed. His smile quickly faded. I followed his gaze out the window. He spent more and more time peering out at the world rather than studying. Sometimes he disappeared into long trances, staring into the void and moving his lips without making a sound. I worried about him.

It had surprised me when James had detected something different in me. He pestered me about some amorous adventure. I assumed these were the musings of a man whose virility had yet to be tested. But he guessed correctly, in part. It did involve a woman. A virgin. Not a woman from the brothels. How ironic: the love I had experienced since my visit to the cathedral came not at the hands of a lover, but from the embrace of a mother.

Ever since I had confessed to the Blessed Mary, I noticed the colors radiating in the Jesuit gardens outside our classrooms. The bees, dragonflies, and butterflies cheered my spirits. My own mother had even reappeared. Memories long lost snuck up on me in broad daylight. She brightened my daydreams. She had never abandoned me; it was I who had banished her. Now I was free again to imagine that she had crossed the ocean to join me here. As she fluttered about campus, a beautiful butterfly, she encouraged me. She sensed that her son's life had purpose.

I returned to my notebook to review the day's teachings while James drifted off. Our other classmates stayed out until the last possible moment. I relished those slices of solitude. With pillows stuffed behind me, I sat up in bed and read by the single light on my bedside table. In this tranquil setting, I detected the presence of nature: the buzz of cicadas, the bark of a lonely dog, or the muffled sound of rain. I wanted to bottle up this serenity, lost when modernity arrived in Bangkok. I savored this lullaby accompanying my bedtime reading.

Although I should have been doing homework, I reached for a book. My reading pleasure had multiplied with my growing access to books. Every time I took out my favorite, I held it to my nose and breathed in. The musty smell evoked the passage of time. My book had traveled from far away; so had I. My eyes caressed the faded, blue cover and worn, green spine. I turned to the title page: *The Poor Man's Prayer: The Story of Credit Union Beginnings*, by George Boyle. I loved the feel of the textured paper. In a ritual that brought me pleasure, I ran my index finger down the new page and flattened it against the spine.

I reread the preface. Although I knew it by heart, I took in each word — perhaps for the hundredth time. When I reached the beginning of the last paragraph, my eyes left the page and I recited the words from memory.

"His adventure was in the field of values and ideas. His master theme was that all men have a social duty. He called it an everlasting duty. The span of 30 years since his death only serves to light up the truth of his words. The purpose of this book, then, is that the courageous and achieving dead may live again to cheer on the living. G. B."

I cherished the idea of inheriting a social duty. Perhaps the author, and maybe even Alphonse Desjardins himself, cheered me on from the other side. A smile formed on my lips.

Desjardins created the first "*caisse populaire*" in 1900 with his wife, so the poor people of Canada, his country, could hold on to their homes and farms. It shocked me to learn that Canada, such an advanced country, once had problems similar to Thailand. He realized people could combine their money and borrow from the pool when they needed to. He figured a way for them to do this without having to put up additional collateral as a guarantee. How ingenious!

Imagine, a man from Quebec studied Germany's banking system to find a solution for his own people. Brilliant! He figured out that the best model of credit unions came from poor working-class people instead of the rich or well educated.

I paused and took a deep breath. I needed to slow down. I wanted the story to unfold gently, to absorb how he developed his thinking as well as his practical application. I wished to indulge in the pleasure of reading word by word. But my eyes raced ahead, impatient to reach the final page, the end of the story, the happy ending.

Of course, Canada enjoys a rich and diverse economy, agriculture, mines, and fisheries. But I assumed farmers were farmers all over the world. The conditions of the local peasants in Cagayan de Oro resembled those of my home. Why, then, would the farmers in Canada be better off? They endure the extra troubles of winter and extreme cold. I read on. Desjardins debated the pros and cons of the two systems of credit unions that came about in Germany. His brother, Napoleon, doubted the possibility that poor people could unite to be productive. He argued with Napoleon, then culled the better of the two ideas, to create a better option. He identified the weaknesses and reduced their impact to create a solution adapted to their unique situation. Desjardins grabbed me from across time and pushed me forward.

I wondered what we could create in Bangkok to make it possible for commoners to own small businesses. Thai people brim with ingenuity. They turn a steel bucket into a BBQ, selling roasted pork on bamboo skewers. They fashion planks, rope, and rollers into carts and haul things for hire. They fold dried-out newspapers into bags and sell them. A small loan could mean the difference between survival, and living a life free from the fear of starvation, homelessness, and hopelessness.

What if farmers could rent land and work for themselves? Would that not be better than working for low pay and forcing children out of school and into the workforce? I saw what the rich man saw. Illiteracy breeds distrust. And distrust is detrimental to the collective will. The result is an endless pool of cheap labor. Poverty fosters discouragement. And it suffocates dreams. What hope is there for the poor if they do not trust those who might lead them?

We should rely on what we know. What if a few families rented a small plot to grow tomatoes, onions, and chilies, and sold the excess? Thailand was full of women with large, straw hats who sold produce by the roadside. Suppose the small collective bought a wok. The children could gather branches for a fire. The women could fry up the vegetables with noodles and eggs. In time, they could buy charcoal and sell hot meals in tin bowls. They might add chili oil and beansprouts to their menu. If this went well, they would have enough money to buy a cart. They could own an "on the go" restaurant. They could get new customers. With others backing them, they could buy a scooter with a sidecar and deliver food. Or rent a bit of land, add tables, and build a roadside restaurant to attract regular patrons.

This vision suffered from one major flaw. The people would first have to come together to rent the plot of land. Alone, they could not afford it. Burdened by feeding too many mouths — because children offer them the only hope for survival in their old age — they spin in an endless circle of poverty. Their needs outstripped their ability to earn, save, and guarantee a loan.

Desjardins understood this. He suggested that such a system be launched in a community where *trust* already existed. My mind raced. What if all the parents whose children attended the Angel Center came together? I saw the potential for all of us. We held the means to break out of our cages. By joining together, people could spare the labor of their firstborn, or their second-born, so at least one child in the family could attend school. With one educated child, imagine how the family's fortune would be enhanced. The new generation of wage earners could become important members of the credit unions. *There had to be a way.*

I rearranged the pillows and turned to the next chapter. Desjardins' enthusiasm sprang from the page. He prepared his ideas for a new type of credit union, to present at his first town meeting. As I read, the possibilities seeped into my soul. I was transported to a country far from Asia. I sat in the first row waiting for him to call the meeting to order. I waited to learn — and, maybe later, to do.

***

I could hardly keep still. I sat uncomfortably in Dr. Jakelit's ill-fitting clothes. For the first time, I resented having a family name with a letter at the end of the alphabet, "W." The long-awaited moment had arrived. I was about to receive my graduation certificate. I summoned patience. Twelve names would be called before mine.

I wished James was here. His absence left a hole in my heart. He tried so hard, but in the end, he could not escape the quicksand. Slowly, the readings and lectures consumed him. He cheated on his sleep until he had no energy or desire to study. He rubbed his hands together more vigorously as illness took over his body, then his mind. Perhaps it was a reminder that his hands, at least, still functioned. Perhaps he would be a carpenter, following in his father's shadow. When he collapsed, his family came for him. I hoped shame and guilt did not ferment within his soul. Those ghosts could take up permanent residence in a man's fiber. I thought I would write to him and suggest a visit to the cathedral.

Father Masterson called my name: *Mr. Amporn Wathanavongs*. I covered my damaged right hand with my left. With three steps, I crossed the vast expanse separating the haves and the have-nots. Father Masterson dominated the stage with his presence and his size.

Serenity emanated from Archbishop Camomot, amplifying his small stature. His delicate Filipino frame belied the strength of a teak tree. A red satchel was pinned to his flowing, white robe.

In a voice as soft as a sparrow's, he chirped, "Congratulation on completing your training. May God bless you." He held my diploma.

I reached for it with my good hand. Lowering my eyes, I clutched my certificate and nodded thank you. My gratitude required no voice. I vowed to satisfy my indebtedness to whatever destiny had brought Father Bonningue into my life. I headed back to my seat, searched the proud faces in the audience. Among them, I saw my mother and father. Here I was, their only child, receiving a diploma. Sunlight streamed into the room. My heart was near bursting. The Blessed Mother Mary smiled upon her son.

When the ceremony ended, I found a bench under the trees in the Jesuit gardens. With great care, I unrolled my diploma.

The birds as my audience, I read it aloud:

South East Asia Rural Social Leadership Institute
SEARSOLIN of Xavier University
This is to certify that AMPORN
WATHANAVONGS has completed the course
of studies and fieldwork in social leadership
and rural development techniques presented
by the Faculty of the South East Asia Rural
Social Leadership Institute and is qualified for
the position of trust in organizations for social
betterment and is hereby granted this TRAINEE
CERTIFICATE.
Cagayan de Oro, Philippines
Awarded this 15th of May, 1965
Reverend William F. Masterson, S.J., Director
Reverend Cornelius J. Quirke, S.J., President

I imagined brilliant feathers of emerald, turquoise, purple, sky blue, and gold fanning around me. On this occasion, I allowed myself to bask in my pride.

***

The announcement blasted from the airport intercom: "Flight 016 to Bangkok, ready for boarding."

Twelve months before when I left Bangkok, life had been so full of uncertainty about my family's survival. The risk of gambling with my own children's welfare was part of every breath I took during my year in Cayagan de Oro. Upon my departure, I could breathe freely. I had gambled and won. I had beaten the odds.

My bag held the same articles on my way home and two new and very special items: my SEARSOLIN certificate and my copy of *The Poor Man's Prayer*. Desjardins had to travel back to Thailand with me to spread his vision of credit unions. With Father Bonningue, we could find a unique Thai solution. I could fulfill my social duty.

"Last call for Flight 016 to Bangkok."

I grabbed my bag and marched down the gangway. In a few short hours, I would be reunited with Sunee and my children. The most precious graduation gift was waiting for me at home. My son, Piak, would read to me. *My son.*

CHAPTER TWENTY-ONE

FATHER BONNINGUE walked into the library and cleared his throat. The morning sun drifted in with him. I lifted my head from the stack of forms I had been filling out.

"*Sawadee* Amporn, or should I say *Bon matin*."

After rubbing the sleep from my eyes, I stretched my arms. The clock read 7:00 a.m. I had had four hours of luxurious sleep.

"I should probably send you home to your family. It is a good thing that we are both men, or your wife might suspect that you have a girlfriend. You are spending too much time here, *mon ami*." He chuckled and handed me a cup of tea.

"*Kob kun krap*. Father Bonningue."

"It is almost like the old days. Remember when you and Sunee lived here? Now you have a family and a mission. Are you ready?"

My voice quivered.

"Yes."

"*Parfait*. Perfect. I will announce this Easter Sunday that the first meeting will take place next Sunday after Mass."

I nodded and returned to my papers. For what felt like the hundredth time, I reviewed each line, looking for errors.

Almost a full month had passed since I had returned from SEARSOLIN. But I had not been idle. Father Masterson had instilled in us a call to action. He had repeated that our time at Xavier should propel us into action when we returned home. He required each of us to complete a development action plan. When he explained that this was to be our personal mission when we rejoined our communities, I knew what mine would be. I pulled out my tattered copy of *Poor Man's Prayer* and vowed to walk in Desjardins' footsteps.

First, I enlisted Father Bonningue. I convinced him that we could launch the first credit union of Thailand in his parish. What better place than the slums east of Bangkok? He blessed my action plan with his usual response: "But of course." Since my return from the Philippines, I noticed that he favored English for our conversations.

I stacked all the books on basic accounting that I could find in the Angel Center library. Although I no longer worked there, once again, the library had become my refuge. With each sunrise, my confidence grew. After two weeks, I had gathered enough notes and additional practical knowledge to create the basic documents to operate a credit union.

When my knowledge failed, my enthusiasm filled in the gaps. Where my resources fell short, Father Bonningue summoned support. Sister Frances Xavier Bell became my new best ally. Teaching at the Mater Dei School in

Bangkok, she spent her time between classes helping me harness the clunky mimeograph machine. As I spun the handle, she caught the copies. More than once, ink traveled onto our fingers and faces. I caught her wiping her hands on her black serge habit. Because she had rolled back the bothersome wide sleeves, ink invariably stained her arms.

She never complained. On the contrary, she took her turn handling the machine. I guessed she was 10 years my senior but her spirit danced with youthfulness. During our copying sessions, she told me a few stories about growing up in Brooklyn and entering the Ursuline novitiate. She educated me in their philosophy. I loved to hear that the Ursulines valued the education of young women. She enjoyed her missionary work in Thailand and vowed to stay for a long time. I hoped so, as her cheerfulness bolstered my confidence.

We bundled each batch of documents: deposit slip, cash disbursement form, passbook and internal administrative paperwork consisting of cash journal, general ledger and balance sheet. I kept them simple. People in the slums distrusted paper, mostly because few could read. But I knew they would trust Father Bonningue and me.

***

Father Bonningue ended Mass with his usual blessing of the parishioners "Amen." He closed his Bible but did not blow out the candles. Martial law was in effect and prohibited more than four people from gathering in public places to hold meetings. People in the slums trusted Father Bonningue, his work, the Jesuits and especially the Angel Center. So they stayed under the pretense of extended Bible studies. But we all kept a watchful eye on the candle, praying it would not go out and that the closed door would not open.

"My dear parishioners, as you know, Amporn has been away for some time learning how to help us improve our living conditions. He has returned with some ideas of how to help us help each other. I ask that you listen to his ideas. Together, with the grace of God, we can serve our community so that your children will have a better life."

I stuck my hands in my pockets. I counted around 150 people. The slums continued to sprawl and put more demands on the Angel Center. It created hope, but would that be enough for the people to trust me, to trust one another? My mouth felt dry.

Father Bonningue waved to me. It took me a moment to find my legs. I took a deep breath and whispered to myself: *Alphonse Desjardins, give me strength, I follow in your footsteps*.

"*Sawadee. Kob kun*. Hello, Thank you for this opportunity to talk with you."

I *wei*-ed to them and bowed my head, low enough for them to grasp my respect for them.

"When I was in the Philippines, I washed and cleaned shirts to make enough money to eat. But I know that for many of you, buying a shirt is not possible. You have to agree to pay 1 *baht* per day to some vendor for a full month so he will give you a 15 *baht* shirt at the end of the month. And that is if you never miss a payment. If you do, you lose all your money.

"That is wrong. They tell you that because you do not have 15 *baht* at one time, they must charge you double the price because they take a risk on you. But when you pay twice as much for something, then you do not have money enough for food. You want a job and you need a shirt.

"We can stop this nightmare. We can come together and save, and we can borrow from each other. Because we are neighbors, because we trust one another to pay the money back …"

As I spoke, some of the people leaned forward. One or two of them nodded. For the next 40 minutes, I explained to them the next steps. When the candle began to flicker, I brought the meeting to an end.

"Well done, Amporn. You were very convincing. I think they will come back and participate," said Father Bonningue, who took my hand and then pulled me in for a hug.

***

"What should I do? I thought all 75 people who came to our second meeting would stay tonight."

I spoke to Father Bonningue under my breath so no one heard us. After Mass had ended, everyone left, except for 13 people who were standing close to the door.

"Amporn, how many people must you have?"

"I think if we have enough people to form a board, we can go ahead. I don't really know. I never imagined so many would give up."

I sighed and avoided thinking about Desjardins.

"Go ahead. You have come this far. Just begin here, where you are, with the people who are willing to follow. In time, others will come. If we help one family, we have made progress."

I remembered Father Masterson. How he had told us it would not be easy. He had urged us to implement our development action plan regardless of the obstacles.

"This is for you Father Masterson," I whispered to myself.

We spent the next two hours electing a board of directors, a loan committee and a supervisory board, the pillar of our credit union. We also appointed an education committee to spread knowledge of the workings of the credit union. Eleven of the 13 held offices. I was elected treasurer to the board of directors, a vote of confidence.

Every founding member paid a membership fee of 10 *baht,* which constituted the central fund of the credit union. We collected another 230 *baht* to be deposited as savings into our account. This money belonged to the individual members. Our total funding amounted to 360 *baht*. It was a start.

On that quiet Sunday evening of July 25, 1965, we officially established the *Soon Klang Thewa* Credit Union (Angel Center Credit Union). The first credit union in Thailand was born. We had succeeded. I thought of Desjardins and said a private "thank you" for cheering me on from the other side, just as George Boyle had promised in his preface to my favorite book.

CHAPTER TWENTY-TWO

MY BLACK tea remained untouched on the kitchen table. The children had left for school. The thought of looking for a new job soured my mood. My lips pursed in self-disapproval. Nine years had passed since I graduated from SEARSOLIN. Nine years had passed since Father Bonningue and I had created the first credit union. I tried to reason with myself that working in a Bangkok office for the last few years had outweighed scraping by. Yet, I realized that for all the knowledge of my new diploma, I was still naïve. I grasped theories and formulas with ease, but the ways of society continued to baffle me.

I glanced around our small home and recalled how I had found it. For seven years, I filled out applications for apartments in a government housing project. They sprouted all over the city—five-story buildings, 20 units each level, rent of 300 *baht* a month per family. No matter how many forms I filled out, we were denied every time. We lived in a rented room with another family who needed extra income more than space. Our shared quarters made factory dormitories appear luxurious. Both families accommodated each other. Poverty builds tolerance beyond reason.

The problem was one of simple economics: supply and demand. The small pool of middle-class families, the Bangkok elite, sought favors from their connections. Even so, their demands outnumbered the supply. Unaware of the inner workings of city politics, I was confounded by rejection after rejection. I had believed the government spokesperson who had told me the projects were intended for low-income families. My income fitted squarely in the low end of the "low" category. It could barely support my family's growing needs. Because I had an office job, I assumed we were an obvious choice for housing. I could have been counted on to pay the rent on time. It never occurred to me that thousands upon thousands of other employed city dwellers were also applying for housing. Only those who understood and played the game were eventually granted an apartment.

I took the rejection personally. The black cloud reappeared. Good fortune had brought me Father Bonningue, Dr. Jakelit, SEARSOLIN, Father Masterson, and my first real job without any maneuvering on my part. Ignorance was the cause of my situation. I had learned to survive in the countryside but was unsophisticated in the ways of the city.

For the first time, I realized Bangkok thrived on an intricate web of connections and favors owed and returned. Who you knew trumped knowledge, education, and skills. Influence was bestowed on those born into the right families, and they mixed with other right families. This group admitted no one from the outside. The next strata consisted of servants, cleaners, and others employed by the "right people." The servants used their contacts skillfully and manipulated them into smaller favors. The rest of us dangled without safety nets. We were just above the vast pit of expendable humans living in the slums.

I smirked. How stupid I still was. I used to think all I needed was a degree and a job to be admitted into society. My trajectory would stop unless I learned to play the game. The black cloud oppressed me. I recalled Father Bonningue's words, "God's will for you." It gave me the courage to go on.

Almost three years ago, when I was working at the United States Air Force (USAF) base, I received a request from the AAFES (US Army and Air Force Exchange Service). It came about when an expatriate arrived from Texas to head up the food branch on the base. He asked me to help him find an experienced secretary fluent in English. It was a reasonable request, given my position as section chief of personnel management. I knew finding someone with such qualifications would be a challenge. He had requested the rarest but most in-demand skills in this part of the world. Because it was his first posting in Asia, he did not know it yet.

A few days later, a Thai woman in her late twenties walked into my office looking for employment. She possessed those rare skills and had experience. While living in the United States, married to an American soldier, she had held a secretarial position. The marriage had failed — cultural differences, she claimed. She had a letter of recommendation from her uncle. I hired her immediately, pleased with my solution for the Texas executive.

Soon after she was employed by him, she came by to express her gratitude, and asked if there was anything she or her uncle, the director general of the Government Housing Bureau, could do for me. I bored her with my woes. I told her I was losing hope of finding proper housing for my family. Then I asked for her advice. Two days later, I received a call from the Government Housing Department. My application had been granted. Keys and a lease were waiting for me.

I could hardly believe it. Perhaps I had outwitted the black cloud. But I knew then, as I do now, depression blows in with a will of its own. After we moved into the new apartment and heard other tenants' stories, I knew we all lived in the debt of someone else's gratitude or in fear of having overleveraged someone's weakness.

The sound of Sunee washing the breakfast dishes drew me back to the moment and my somber mood. I avoided telling her about the Air Force base closing. Unless I could find a new job, we risked losing our home. Sunee reminded me of a sparrow. She was happy to make do with little. She spread joy while moving about the house. She may have been small in stature, but she defended her own with a powerful beak. Her tender heart spoiled our children, allowing them extra moments of peaceful sleep. She would make their beds and wash their dishes. The children long ago had forgotten the restless nights of another time — when they all shared one bed which was too crowded and too hard, in a tumble-down shack unable to stand up to Mother Nature. I had learned that children were resilient. But Sunee remembered those long nights. She still worried about the children and felt guilty for the times they had had to do without. What she failed to see, was that she had won that battle long ago.

My children were well adjusted. They had only faint memories of their early days. Piak and Ampol wrestled over their favorite soccer ball. Toum pouted in the practiced manner of an adorable little girl denied a second serving of sweet bread. Tata, our last-born child, displayed limitless stubbornness when her homework needed attention. They obliged me with gratifying moments of family life. My greatest joy was the knowledge that their childhood would be filled with laughter, ice cream, drawings, swims, and a few scratched knees. I vowed to find the strings to pull this all together. We would stay in our house. I would shelter Sunee from my worries. She had done more than her part.

Once again, I turned to the employment section of the *Bangkok Post*. The ads never changed: hotel staff, construction workers, and house-cleaning staff wanted. My old foe, uncertainty, was lodged between my rib cage and my heart. No steps back this time. I needed to figure out where the real jobs were advertised.

Filled with frustration, I almost missed the ad seeking managerial skills:

Christian Children's Fund (CCF) looking for Thai National for a program manager position. CCF is a nongovernmental agency, based in the United States with operations around the world. Our mission is to develop the quality of life of marginalized and disadvantaged children; provide educational opportunities for children in need; enhance the potential of families to support children's well-being. If you possess a master's degree in social work or equivalent experience, are fluent in English, please consider joining our organization to make a difference.

***

"Good morning, Mr. Wathanavongs. Thank you for coming. Take a seat, please."

The man gestured to the chair on the other side of his desk.

"You are not our traditional candidate. Normally, our candidates hold a master's degree in social work, an MSW, and a recommendation from the nonprofit organizations where they've worked."

Stacks of papers, pencils, and pens shared space with a black telephone on his desk. He must have been important. Something was familiar about his face. Bangkok's people tended to keep within their own restricted circles. Rarely did they mix. But we had met before, I was sure of it.

Then, I remembered. I wondered if he did. We had met over nine years ago through Bishop Clarence James Duhart, the first Redemptorist bishop of Udon Thani, in the north, near Laos. I worked at the Angel Center then. I was pretty certain that he was the priest who had been working for the Catholic Relief Services. How could I forget him? He had a German build, angular face, broad forehead, big bones, wide shoulders, and hands to catch fish without a pole or net. It puzzled me how, with such a physique, he spoke American English.

I remember asking him for typewriters to help us with training programs for the mothers at the Angel Center. He had donated five. I saw him a few other times in the early days, when Father Bonningue and I were approaching Catholic churches for help to promote the credit unions.

He interrupted my visit into the past.

"Let me tell you about the Christian Children's Fund, which we shorthand to CCF," he said looking straight at me.

This American habit of visual directness intimidated me. I feared he may detect the difficult road I had traveled, the way a distorted image reflects on water.

"I'm looking for someone who can get things done.

Someone practical; not someone just full of theory. The people back home, at the head office in Richmond, Virginia, generally don't interfere with what I'm doing. That's because I get the job done. I need someone who can help me deliver results."

He scratched the back of his neck, and his face contorted into an expression of annoyance.

"I apologize for hogging the conversation. It's my bad habit. I talk too much. I want to hear about you and why you are interested in working for us."

He stood up. "I'm sorry, I forgot to introduce myself."

He extended his meaty hand. We shook. His hand buried mine. I was taken aback by his directness and the firmness of his grasp.

"My name is Anthony Tersch, although everyone calls me Tony. I'm the national director for Thai operations. I moved from Chicago to Thailand several years ago. My mother was from Austria, which explains this healthy paunch." He patted his stomach. "I was a Catholic missionary priest in Thailand, part of the Redemptorist Order. That was a long time ago. Now I am married to a wonderful Thai woman."

I struggled over whether to disclose our previous association. I hesitated. I feared triggering some past misfortunes, which he might project onto me. Better to wait.

"Here I go again, doing all the talking. I'm incorrigible." The man chuckled.

What was so funny? Having no idea, I decided to change the subject.

"Pleased to meet you, sir. My name is Amporn Wathanavongs."

"Please call me Tony."

"And you may call me Amporn."

Tony nodded and settled back into his chair. He reminded me of a bear.

"Amporn, I see here you worked for a number of companies. Please describe each of your positions. Also, why did you change jobs?"

I wondered if I would be able to speak.

"Yes, it would be my pleasure. I graduated in 1965 from SEARSOLIN, with a diploma in Social Development from the Agricultural College of Xavier University in the Philippines." I paused to catch my breath.

"I'm familiar with it. It's run by the Jesuits. They believe in good education and actually do something about it."

"Yes, I agree. I learned a lot that year about the strength of collective unions for rural people. The collectives increase efficiency and build support systems to overcome crises. Also, these community organizations form a basis of learning. Children enjoy clean places to play, and the parents are taught new skills. The real challenge lies in convincing people to care for those outside their own family, and a willingness to pull together for the benefit of the community. Eventually, everyone gains something."

"What happened after you came back from the Philippines? Why didn't you return to the Angel Center? Why did you go into the private sector? You could have applied your knowledge at the Angel Center."

I shifted in my seat. I was certain he had forgotten our past meeting.

"Well, sir, er, Tony, I worked at the Angel Center for four years before I went to study. At first I did whatever was needed. Over time, I began doing social work without knowing what social work was. I was responsible for organizing educational programs for children and training for adults. I visited homes to help families find ways to care for their children and to support themselves. Those families struggled very hard, Mr. Tersch — Tony."

"But after getting your diploma, you gave this up. Why?"

I studied my polished shoes while wrestling with the real answer. Would he think ill of me if I told him I needed to make more money? I wanted a better, more comfortable life for my family.

"When I left for the Philippines, I was replaced at the Angel Center. When I returned, I continued to volunteer nights and weekends for two years. It was my way of thanking Father Bonningue — he was the Jesuit brother in charge — for all his support. But please understand, my first priority was to improve my family's situation after my year-long absence. Our financial situation was in crisis. My family was living in poverty. I had promised my wife we would be much better off when I returned."

I resisted telling him how much I had always wanted to work for a company in Bangkok, follow regular hours, and be greeted politely when I walked into an office. That I believed I could use my mind rather than my hands to earn a living. I wanted to wake up every morning knowing I was providing well and had become a good father.

For the first time, I noticed Tony was not wearing a jacket.

"I found an ad for a position in the newspaper." I doubted Tony appreciated how proud I felt searching for a position in the *Bangkok Post*. I assumed he was highly educated to work overseas and would not understand.

I continued: "I was hired as the office manager by an Indian-based drug company, Unichem."

He interrupted me. "I see that you worked there only two years."

Was he accusing me of something? I felt jittery. I inhaled slowly to steady my voice.

"Then you went to the US Air Force base. That's an interesting career change, Amporn."

Tony lowered his head and peered at me over the rim of his glasses. His eyes bored into me. I wondered whether they taught all Catholic priests this technique. I remembered Father Masterson doing the same. Did they think we would speak a greater truth if they peered at us over their glasses?

I tightened my grip on the armrest. "Calm down, calm down." I reasoned with myself. He was American. I worked at an American base. He would appreciate my efforts.

"Tony, there is a story behind this. Should I share it with you, or would you prefer to hear about my responsibilities at U-Tapao Air base?"

"I like stories," Tony said. "Please go on."

"You see, the first Thai credit union was created in 1965, with its seat at the Angel Center. It was called the *Soon Klang Thewa* Credit Union. Father Bonningue found some funding and I helped him create the organization. After my studies at SEARSOLIN, I wanted to help rural people find ways to create small businesses. Noodle carts or selling goods at the market — anything, really — machetes or pots, even coal. The villagers require basic financial support to start a business. They have no, what do you call this extra cash?"

"Disposable income," said Tony as he leaned forward.

"Yes. They are so poor, no one will trust them with a loan. We wanted to give them small loans. Sometimes $ 5 was enough for them to get started. We wanted to teach them to not spend everything they had on food, even if they were starving. It was difficult to make them understand the idea of using money to make money. To them, money was for three things: food, clothes, and making merit at the temples."

Tony nodded. "I understand."

"It took a while for them to realize, if they put their money into a small home business, they could earn a regular wage. When things were good, if they put a few *baht* aside, it would be there for when they needed it, for emergencies. The most important part was to be regular, consistent, in the goods they sold and the services they provided. Some were successful. They would hide the extra money, usually burying it in the garden. The next step was a lot harder, teaching them to trust the credit union to keep their money safe. I suspect few understood it was *their* saved money creating the loans for others. They began to trust their bank, thinking their money was in the bank building. They came together to establish a small credit union. I was so excited to see the effects on the village. It was not theory to me anymore, it was real."

He jumped in.

"Yes, yes. I understand how credit unions function. But how is this relevant?"

"While I was employed by Unichem, I took courses on credit unions from the international arm of the Credit Union National Association, CUNA. It is based in the United States. Are you familiar with it?" I asked.

"No. Were you so busy with these courses you neglected your responsibilities and were fired?"

"No, not at all. But I did change jobs because of my involvement with credit unions. In November 1967, the International Labour Organization sponsored a conference in Hong Kong. I was asked to be a representative at the Asian Seminar on the International Federation of Christian Trade Unions. It was a month-long event. The owners of the drug company were reluctant to give me time off, but in the end, they agreed to let me participate. The conference fascinated me. Then, I was asked to speak about the labor workers' situation in Thailand."

Tony fidgeted with some papers on his desk. "Go on."

"After that, things became complicated."

He held my résumé in his hands and gave me his full attention.

"OK. Why was it complicated?"

"I was nervous about telling the truth about the situation in Thailand. I contacted the director general of the Department of Labor in Bangkok and received authorization to speak frankly. So I talked about the meager salary of manual workers and the unsafe working conditions. I told how people were forced to live in squalor and toil longer hours than water buffaloes. I mentioned the laws prohibiting workers from having meetings to discuss their situation. I suppose I said too much."

I paused, recalling my speech. I had been calm in front of hundreds of people. It was unbelievable. They were listening to me, to what I had to say. I told them everything I knew. Some alarms went off in my head, but the experience was so powerful, I ignored them. I had found my voice.

"I don't know if you were in Thailand in the late 1950s. That was the time of General Sarit's martial rule. He had outlawed all trade unions in 1957. When I went to Hong Kong 10 years later, he was still ruling and his government had not grown any fonder of unions."

Tony dropped my résumé. His mouth was agape.

"I was here then, but I was a priest," he said. "I focused on my mission and generally avoided government and politics. We believe in the division of State and religion."

I did not understand what he meant. Rather than ask and reveal my ignorance, I went on.

"I didn't expect that speaking at a Hong Kong conference about Thai labor conditions would echo all the way to Bangkok. That's when my problems started. When I landed in Bangkok, police followed me from the airport. On the way to my house, they stopped me and took me to the police headquarters. They questioned me for hours on my involvement with the unions and the Communists. Who did I associate with? Which courses had I taken? Why did I take them? Were there plans to reorganize unions in Thailand?"

I bit my lower lip, unsure of how much more should I disclose. I believed my actions had been correct. Eventually, from all the stretching, the fabric rips. Something compelled me to tell Tony everything. I intuitively trusted him.

"I had no knowledge of the union movement in Thailand, or even if there was one. I want you to understand, I was not mistreated, but it was frightening to be held by the police and asked questions for hours. I was keenly aware I had no one to call to rescue me or give me money to pay my way out of any trouble. Eventually, they drove me home. But the police followed me everywhere —from my home to the company, from the company to the Angel Center, from the Angel Center back to my home. The owners of the drug company grew uneasy. Their papers were in order to operate a foreign company. But police cars on your doorstep are not exactly a good luck charm for business."

Tony nodded. I thought he wanted me to continue.

"One morning when I came in, one of the owners, Mr. K. A. Prao, said to me, 'Mr. Amporn, we value your work very much. However, we loathe two people showing up every day for your job: you and the police. We suggest you find new employment.' I had no choice but to leave. It was difficult. This was my first real job. Everything was progressing smoothly in my life and my family was content, but I understood their concerns."

"That's when you found work with the United States Air Force (USAF) base?" Tony asked.

"Yes. There was a lot of talk about Communists then. I thought the police would leave me alone if I worked there. They would assume the Americans would not hire anyone with Communist beliefs, especially at their own air force base."

Tony chuckled. He looked very amused.

"Clever. Did they leave you alone?"

"Yes. They stopped following me. I felt better. My family felt better, too. I was very happy to lose this shadow. I had a few good years. They appointed me manager at the supply store for the army personnel. They offered me courses. I enjoy studying, so I took advantage of this. I received some training in personnel management. I challenged myself to implement what they taught me. They recognized my efforts and promoted me."

I paused to relive the satisfaction. Recognition of one's accomplishments nurtures self-worth. For a street child robbed at birth of self-esteem, this nourishes the seed of possibility. If it happens a few times, the seed might find root. Mine had, more than once.

"Congratulations. You must have performed well," he said.

Tony's smile grew into a grin.

He rejoiced in my good news, shared my victory. Missionaries, priests, Jesuits, Redemptorists, they were men of great character.

"I moved up to the position of assistant to the section chief of personnel. I was very excited to finally work in a Bangkok office. I wore a tie and close-toed shoes. People had to respect me. I was the person who held the section chief's schedule."

"What was your role there?" Tony asked.

"I was responsible for hiring almost 1000 employees in and around Bangkok. It was difficult to find the best people. Sometimes I had a lot of pressure to hire someone with connections. I wanted the best person, but I had to bow to others. How do you say it? I had to get the job done. It was impossible to fight favoritism, especially if I could not find another good candidate. Few people in this country have the opportunity of getting a university education. Those who do are usually privileged."

Tony looked me in the eye. I returned his gaze. It was a bold move on both our parts. Finding myself at ease, my posture straightened. I kept myself in check, careful not to show off too much colorful plumage. A flashback placed me in the *kutti* next to *Phra* Teacher. It warned me that pride is a sly acquaintance.

"So, why did you leave?"

"With the Vietnam War over, I knew it was only a matter of time before the Americans packed up and went back home. Last week, they finally told me they will close down the remaining operations next year, so I should start to look for a new job."

"Your search has ended, Amporn." Tony got up and opened his door.

"*Khun* Sonthaya and *Khun* Srisak, please come into my office. Let me introduce you to our new childcare coordinator."

CHAPTER TWENTY-THREE

ON THE public bus rumbling over dirt roads in the Ubon region of northeast Thailand, I sank my teeth into a steaming, bamboo-stuffed bun. I had lost track of the number of villages I had visited. I was on a mission. Our head office had informed us that some benefactors in Hong Kong were willing to sponsor 200 or 300 children through the Christian Children's Fund (CCF). Tony worked diligently to ensure Thailand would be among the top recipients of this aid. The offer was extended to 27 regional offices. Until Hong Kong ran out of money, it would grant the funds on a first-come-first-served basis, upon presentation of proper documentation.

"Amporn, I want you out in the field. You and I know the area around the northeast border suffers from the greatest poverty. We have no offices there. You must go in person. Find some local authorities, I don't care who they are. Identify the kids, prepare case histories, and figure out how to cooperate with these agencies to sponsor the children. This forms the core of our mission. This is what I hired you for. I am counting on you."

I bounced in my seat over the bumpy roads. The ride reminded me of my days with the credit unions. It stirred my call to social duty that George Boyle wrote about. What I was doing here, in this remote part of my own country, gave meaning to my past. All the hungry children I saw, diminished by their condition, carried shame in their eyes. It may have been mixed with innocence and playfulness, but their hunger was always present. It said, "I am not good enough to have a full belly." It called to Lek, my fragile, hungry, boyish self.

I carried a suitcase full of papers with names, ages, family histories, addresses, and other details, which I had highlighted. Paperwork, especially this type of foreign form, required specific information. The countryside had no use for this. I overlooked the hesitation and the distant gazes of the people providing me with answers; I did not question them further. These children were real and their hunger was real. If there was a chance of finding them sponsors, then the facts were real. In this part of the world, details and memories were often buried or forgotten. I had been working with CCF for two years, and every child was the sibling I never had. Every child held my beginning. I wanted to offer each and every one a different journey.

Khun Jettrin, the local representative of the regional Ministry of Agriculture, sat behind me on the van.

"In this town, at least 10 children are below the age of five," he said.

I found it impossible to concentrate on his words. I was hanging onto the handle over the seat and doing my best to twist around to hear him. The driver must have imagined himself in a racing car. The van screeched around the curves, voicing its displeasure. Fortunately, the road wound along rice fields instead of ravines. *God, please keep us safe.*

"Who cares for the children?" I asked.

Before he could answer, I was forced against the dashboard. My left arm instinctively went to my head. Pain in my left side propelled me into the jungle. Then I passed out.

***

"Tony, this is not funny. I have been lying bruised in a hospital bed for two weeks. I look like a *muay* Thai boxer who lost the big fight. I have a broken left arm and a black eye. Between the martial curfews and the lack of gasoline, I can hardly believe they got me to Singburi village," I shouted into the hospital director's telephone.

He kindly stepped out of his office to give me privacy.

"Amporn, you are like a cat. You enjoy nine lives. The war didn't kill you, you survived suicide attempts, and now you walk away from a van accident. What are you complaining about?"

He infuriated me. This was not an appropriate time for humor. I regretted telling him the details of my life. Those who rarely suffer misfortune embellished the virtues of adversity.

"Tony, I will get back to the office in a week. I promise. This is not my fault. The reports will be ready in time. Please, I want to keep my job."

"And this worries you? Don't worry. You still have six lives left, more than enough to get you to retirement."

I bit my tongue. He had become a good friend in the last few years, but he was still my boss.

"Anything else?"

"Yes, the staff would appreciate an order of *khanom pia*, the pork-flavored buns. We know you are getting fat on local Chinese delicacies. Get yourself back here."

I hung up the phone. My anger melted into gratitude.

***

The ritual of enjoying my morning tea and taking a few moments to reflect on the new day had begun at the Angel Center. It was a luxury for those living well, a pleasure not afforded to those who were struggling to survive. I had reached those ranks. I inhaled the aroma of jasmine. A blend of gratitude and joy warmed me. My work at CCF brought me a sense of satisfaction that was different from my previous jobs.

My eyes wandered to the photo of Tony and me in Chiang Mai, surrounded by children attending school. I loved looking at this photo that I kept on the credenza near my desk. It broadcasted joy. Well-fed, the children played and learned to read and write. They knew poverty — and they knew dignity. It took so little: a bowl of noodles, a place to develop their minds, and a family to go home to at night.

Tony and I smiled along with the children. Of course, we looked younger then. The picture was taken almost 10 years before on one of my first up-country trips. I remember thinking, at the time, how poverty reached every cracked noodle bowl and dirt patch in my country, no matter how close or far away from Bangkok. Back then, what I learned in the Philippines sounded so logical, practical, and easy to implement. All it required was leadership and effort. Father Bonningue had provided the first and I had given the second. I recalled our early success with the credit union.

Everything seemed possible then, but reality proved to be far more complex. The power structure and the concentration of economic wealth among a few was no accident. It took me a long time to realize that those at the top wanted this economic model to continue. The rich were no different from the vendors at the Surin market. They would rather let the unsold vegetables spoil than give them to people who were starving.

A country is underdeveloped when its resources, including its people, are untapped. The concentration of power in the hands of the few creates a large, renewable pool of cheap and uneducated labor. It also cultivates a society dulled to human suffering and enslaved to their luxuries, especially ones that project the appearance of power.

CCF did what the conscience of the elite tried to squelch. It rekindled hope. With food and education, dreams were reborn. Dreams feed courage. CCF kept growing. It would never run out of people to care for. For the first time in my life, I felt secure. I was making a difference.

We moved our Bangkok offices from 7 Sukhumvit Road to a more spacious location at number 33. With 25 staff sharing an office, we needed more room. Thailand was not the only Southeast Asian country struggling with poverty. I applied what I had learned in my country elsewhere. I coordinated programs in the Philippines, Indonesia, and Sri Lanka. I worked internationally from our local office. What continually amazed me was that people halfway around the world — Italy, France, the United Kingdom, the United States, Canada, Australia, and Sweden — cared enough to do something about the poverty in our relatively small region. Some gave money and others gave their time. People like Tony gave their lives to improve the conditions of people for whom they had no responsibility. A different compass guided their journey.

Tony touched a special place in my heart. At first he was only my boss, but over the years he had become my mentor and a close friend. Tony would retire very soon. I feared the place would be off-kilter for a long while. I would miss our conversations and his odd sense of humor.

Tony and I were like fencers. I presented an idea, for example, serving milk to the children during school. Tony riposted. I was then on the defense. He challenged me until I found solutions to his every attack. When he ran out of reasons why my idea would not work, he championed the plan and facilitated with the head office. Sometimes the home office in Virginia implemented its own foil and the questions bounced back. When I felt discouraged, Tony's laughter worked its magic and I found my conviction again.

Together, we knew when to push for extra funds, when to stand up for new pilot projects for the region, and when to pull back and wait for a better time. Sometimes we got carried away and forgot that the people in Virginia made the big decisions. We had become used to "making things happen" which is a very American concept Tony had taught me. We had to remind ourselves from time to time that our work would not be possible without the people in Virginia.

They had not selected Tony's replacement. It would be someone competent, I was sure, probably from overseas. One thing was certain: Tony's record here and his love for my country could not be duplicated. It comforted me that he would not leave the country. With his greying mane and growing paunch he looked anything but Thai, yet his heart and tongue were pure Thai.

As if on cue, Tony walked into my office. He had a way of showing up at the right time, keeping my spirits on an even keel. We greeted each other, as we had done thousands of times before.

"Well, this is it, my last day, Amporn," he said. "It's hard to believe. After 14 years with CCF, it's time for me to go. Retirement used to seem a long way off. I'm not complaining. I just hope Dusanee doesn't mind having me at home all the time."

Tony sat across from me, as if we were about to review one of our projects.

The difficulty of his leaving was made easier by knowing my friend would only be a short drive away.

"You know, she is so busy with her job at Proctor & Gamble, my biggest adjustment will be not having someone to talk to all the time."

To imagine Tony not talking was like trying to picture Sunday Mass without a priest. He began talking to me at my interview 10 years ago, and had not stopped.

"I plan to swim every day. Around the corner from my house, there is a hotel with a rooftop pool."

"I've had a good career. With my pension, we can live comfortably here in Bangkok, as long as Dusanee continues to manage our finances. I'm hopeless. It is why I hired people like you, who can make things happen."

Tony loved his wife and their two children, Kayvalyn and Max, profoundly. What would he do at home all day? He had been helping people from the time he was a missionary priest. How could he stop now?

"You know, Tony, you don't have to retire," I said, treading softly.

"What?" Tony looked surprised.

"You have all this experience. You have enough money. Why don't you create your own foundation to help kids in Thailand? You know, the 'Tony Has a Big Heart Foundation.' Soon as I retire, in about 13 years, I'll come work for you. Until then, I can help you in my free time. Imagine all the good you could do. You know so many people, and you would not have to worry about approval from the head office. Although I think from time to time you did enjoy battling with Virginia. Anyway, the first step would be to …"

I got up and paced. "It's not a bad idea," I said. "I could help, just like when I was at the Angel Center."

"Amporn." Tony used a tone I had come to know. It meant "Be quiet."

I went on.

"Maybe Dusanee's company would make a small donation to help get you off the ground."

"Amporn," Tony repeated.

"Yes?"

"I'm retiring. I have two kids and a wife. I don't want to risk my retirement money. All the government approvals, not knowing whether sponsors will follow through, establishing programs from scratch, it's a huge responsibility. It's time for you to carry on. And it's time for me to enjoy my swims and get caught up on American politics."

I backed off.

"Yes, of course, you're right, Tony. It is time for you to slow down, enjoy life, and have more time for your American politics. I am happy for you."

I returned to my chair.

"Tony, I'll miss you."

He had been like the brother I never had.

"I will miss you, Amporn. Hiring you was one of my best decisions. I am counting on you to move CCF forward. The children are counting on you. I fear going into shock from immediate withdrawal. So I want you to keep me informed."

Tony walked over to me. Facing each other, we crossed the Austrian-Thai cultural divide and hugged as brothers.

***

Everyone had gone for the day. Night crept into the office. Sitting in the dark was appropriate to my mood. The local office both infuriated and humiliated me. They decided I lacked the necessary "qualifications" to be the national director. This ploy, to name *Khun* Srisak and me as co-directors until a suitable candidate was found, dripped with condescension. I should have followed *Khun* Srisak's lead and left immediately. She was decisive. She rebuffed their insult. For more than a decade, I had proven myself, delivering positive results. Did they think Tony did it alone? This whole affair reeked of local arrogance. Why did I need more education? The head office had remained silent about this local showdown. I knew how to get the job done. Why should my lack of family connections or formal education matter at this point?

The next day I would have to be polite to Dr. Chitpong. The doctor had a medical degree from Cornell University. This title and his family connections qualified him for the position. It was ridiculous. A man born of and living with privilege, who had never been hungry or held a child dying not from illness, but from hopelessness. Someday, all poor children would have a chance to learn to read and write, like those in the US or Europe. They would go to high school as a right, not a privilege. Some would go on to university. Someday, poor children would not be punished for being born in a hut surrounded by coconuts.

***

Dr. Chitpong never showed up. Office morale waned further. CCF employees felt slighted by the doctor. They feared our local office had cast doubt on their abilities. We all feared their inability to secure an acceptable replacement for Tony would give the head office a convenient reason to shut down our operations. The local board of directors fanned the employees' anxiety by squabbling over who should be the next director. Tony had already been retired for six months. During that time, I had been the "acting" national director. All was running smoothly. It would have been logical to appoint me. I had proven myself time and again. The local board was paralyzed by the thought that someone like me, without a pedigree, should be their choice. They thought it would reflect badly on their social standing.

I had called a general meeting. This was not a common practice, but I needed to do something. This was the first time I had addressed the employees formally as a group, in my capacity as "acting" national director. Sweat beaded on my forehead. The employees looked at me with quizzical expressions. I exaggerated my smile. I learned this technique from Tony. Employees relaxed when they saw the boss smiling. I also learned from him to give praise. Encouragement comes from expressing gratitude for hard work. Everyone enjoys a compliment. I hope they viewed my news in a positive light.

I took a deep breath and began.

"Look at the photos on the wall — all of those laughing children. It is because of each of you that their happiness is possible. Your work is important. It changes people's lives. You should be proud of what you accomplish every day. Not everyone can say that what they do matters. What you do matters, to them, and to me. *Kob kun krap*. Thank you."

The room relaxed. Now I could share my news.

"Before we return to work, I have an announcement to make. This is of a personal nature."

The chatter stopped immediately.

"The people in our head office have asked me to complete a master's of business administration here at Chulalongkorn University in Bangkok."

The employees clapped as if I had just announced bonuses for everyone.

"This will take me about two years. I ask for your patience and support as I try to fulfill my obligations here while studying. Classes will be held every day from five to nine in the evening, so I will need to leave the office early. Unfortunately, I will not be available for weekend events, as I need to attend classes on Saturday and Sunday as well. Please keep this in mind when you are scheduling appointments with me, or events where my attendance is necessary. This will be challenging for all of us. I will have to ask some of you to travel in my place. I want to thank you in advance for your kind support. I will remember this. Hopefully, when I have my degree, all requirements will be satisfied and we can move ahead without uncertainty."

As those last words flew from my mouth, I saw that one of the local board members had slipped into the room. I swallowed hard and hoped he had not heard my last statement. What was he doing here, anyway? I did not expect any board members that day. Maybe he heard about this meeting.

I blocked the anger before it reached my brain so I would not say something I would later regret. On my way home, I thought about the board's obstinacy. Tony had prepared me to be his successor. Head office would have confirmed me. But the local board was dissatisfied with my lack of educational credentials. They could not parade me around as their poster child without a "proper" university degree. It would have demonstrated to the Bangkok elite the board's lack of social clout. Head office, blind to the political implications for the local board members, offered what they perceived as a viable and practical solution — sponsoring me, the "acting" national director, to complete an MBA degree. The move was clever on their part. The board had no choice but to agree to my eventual appointment.

This piece of paper would represent a lifetime membership to a prestigious club. It would provide me entry to places where I had been denied admittance my entire life. Perhaps it was written in the stars or in God's plans for me, but by the time I turned 50 I would graduate. People who wandered among the skyscrapers of Bangkok would finally have to accept me as their peer. The appointment would merely be a formality.

***

The next two years were blurred. I was either studying or working. My presence at family events was rare. I was a spirit inhabiting nowhere. The pressure of always being two steps away from where I should be drained me physically and mentally. My determination to grasp the all-important piece of paper that would admit me as a full member of society, and my vision of belonging, propelled me forward.

On May 22, 1987, I achieved my goal. My name was called. The dean of business for Chulalongkorn University handed me my degree certificate. Standing among much younger classmates, I received my master's in business administration. Looking over the audience, I imagined a blue common jay butterfly floating above the faces I saw. My mother was there with me and she was proud of her son.

***

Still, the board argued about my appointment. Bewildered over this latest roadblock, I cursed my misfortune. The board said I lacked the appropriate background. What they meant was I lacked the proper social standing and family connections. They knew I was not part of their world, their club, and I never would be. Sacrificing and studying for two years had changed nothing for them. Head office grew tired of a battle that baffled them. Caught in a tug-of-war between Richmond and Bangkok, I waited for a resolution. Disagreement deepened. The cultural divide widened. I feared becoming a casualty.

The dispute stirred up years of stored-up hurt. Why was everything I did still not enough? I had a university degree now. I performed my job well. I was bilingual. My employees respected me. Would I be a victim of my birthplace forever? Despite having tried everything to correct my past, it continued to haunt me. I remained and always would be an orphan. I could not reseed my roots.

My title had not changed in the board's views. They would not concede. Head office needed a properly titled head. The board claimed this state of limbo hindered their fund-raising efforts. Amendments to the bylaws required ratification by the local board. A compromise was reached. I was appointed "designate" national director. The donors did not like it. I did not like it either. The battle continued.

In another play of hands, I was finally given the title of national director. But the appointment was conditional on a six month probation period. The board had not lost. I felt like a thief again. Something I had earned was not being freely given.

The months passed uneventfully. Still, I kept expecting to hear that the board had found a new candidate or some other ploy to upend my final appointment. The six months expired. The board had run out of ideas to unseat me.

On November 15, 1987, after a three year struggle, I formally accepted the appointment as national director. The board did not attend the employee-organized celebration. The bitter aftertaste of the *neem* leaf of my homeless youth lingered in my mouth. Nothing could brighten this period of my life. The board had made it clear: I did not belong in their realm.

***

Three years into my official position as national director, King Rama IX gave me what had evaded me: status.

Dear Mr. Wathanavongs,

The King's Palace wishes to inform you that you have been awarded the Royal decoration of the Most Exalted Order of the White Elephant, Member (Fifth Class) to be presented by His Majesty the King for your service to the nation, at the King's Palace in Bangkok on December 5, 1990.

With deep appreciation for your service to the children of the Royal Kingdom of Thailand.

I now belonged to the oldest chivalric order of my country.

Another six years later, in January 1996, the American Coastline University, based in Louisiana, conferred upon me an honorary doctorate in social development. Once again my name changed, this time to Dr. Amporn Wathanavongs.

The privilege of status was now permanently affixed to my name. Perhaps my life was God's will.

CHAPTER TWENTY-FOUR

I FOUND some irony in the fact that Thailand celebrates National Scout Day. Waves of kids in khaki-brown uniforms, with red, green, or yellow scarves and hats flood the streets. King Rama VI, "the father of scouting," had no idea how big the movement would become when he introduced it to my country. Every year on July 1st, Thai schoolchildren, rich or poor, parade and shout their motto: *"Sia cheep ya sia sat."* (Better to die than to lie.) Many of my CCF children participated. I never quite understood how their parents managed to get them the proper uniforms for this event. What sacrifices they have had to endure. But I appreciated that they wanted their children to belong.

For me, that particular National Scout Day, on July 1, 1997, represented a lie. I held unending appreciation for my staff's boundless dedication. I had enjoyed the most fulfilling 10 years of my life as national director of CCF. Gratitude sprang from the part of my heart that loved unconditionally. But on that day, I had to transfer my authority to my successor. And so, I was also besieged with deep melancholy.

Deceit lied at the very root of this day: I had to resign by force of law, by the disgraceful reality that my age dictated my departure, not my free will. The early years of my life were robbed from me. I did not live; I merely survived. I wanted to demand that those years be given back to me so that I could continue my work. But to which greater authority could I appeal?

Head office had given me six months to ease out of a decade of helping children. My protests failed to reach them on the other side of the ocean. This time the cultural differences conspired against me. The American obsession to retire and live the good life mystified me. For me, this was the good life. I could work another quarter century without hesitation. My calendar brimmed with appointments and events. Absent were the black cross marks signifying the number of days until I could swap my suit for a casual *chut tai* traditional Thai shirt and retire … as if reaching a point where you had nothing to do, and nothing was expected of you, should be a cause for celebration. I may have been 60 years old, but I would have been lying if I had said I looked forward to my official retirement on January 1, 1998. I would play no part in making my successor's transition perilous; my staff deserved better. Publically, I commended the smooth changeover but privately I loathed it. I hoped I would not punished for telling a lie. But I was never a Boy Scout.

***

The first day of 1998 felt like a death sentence. I was officially retired. No reason to go to the office. No reason to get up in the morning. I maintained my routine, sat at the kitchen table, sipped my tea, and read the *Bangkok Post*. In truth, I merely browsed the paper, as nothing caught my attention. I used to read articles on the government's economic policy, natural disasters in the provinces, and, of course, any announcement coming from the Department of Education. My eyes skipped over the headlines to stare out of the window. I noticed that the boys had done a good job washing our cars the day before. My Honda Civic and Sunee's Mercedes E220 gleamed in the morning sun. Well, I had managed to give my family a home, security, a comfortable life, and a sense of belonging.

The years of travel and consummate focus on the CCF mission had etched a distance among us. My children exhibited independence. They reserved their thoughts, but their pride showed through when they handed me good school grades. At times, giggles escaped from the living room as they chatted with their mother. We were a family, but my children also shared privileges and comforts that integrated them into a social group of like peers. My wife deserved the home she had created. I derived happiness from the knowledge that they experienced my love through the life I had made possible for them. Their children, my future grandchildren, would be born into a world of possibilities.

Some color returned to my days. I recalled Tony's words when I was stranded up-country, bruised up from the accident. "You still have six lives left, more than enough to get you to retirement." I wondered how many were left now and what shall I do with them.

***

"*Sawadee*, Tony," I said as I walked through the fully opened sliding glass doors leading into Tony's living room.

"Hey. How are you? Or maybe I should ask where have you been? I've lost track with all those lectures, Mr. Successful Alumni. Xavier University must have been proud to welcome you back."

His boundless, jovial nature supported by his solid Austrian build welcomed me. Retirement agreed with Tony. He had adapted without a wrinkle.

"I am fine. A little jet-lagged. I've just returned from Sophia University, in Japan, where I delivered a presentation to Xavier's brother institute."

"Wow, the globetrotter. First your UNICEF tours of Africa and now this. Better you than me. CNN Live brings the world to me, where I want it." Tony patted his worn leather recliner.

"I know, Tony. Maybe it is more than jet lag. Maybe I am tired of running around but not doing anything real. Oh, it's nice to travel, most of the time business class, too. But for what? The drive to act, to make a difference, still eats away at me."

"I thought that's why you started Amporn Consulting, to set all the NGOs straight, shape them up, and get them to work more efficiently. That sounds pretty hands-on to me." Tony adjusted the lever on his beloved recliner.

Dusanee walked in. "Good afternoon, *Khun* Amporn. Nice to see you. Would you like some tea?"

"*Sawadee*, *Khun* Dusanee. That would be lovely. I've come to see if I can get Tony away from his television so we can work together again."

Her eyebrows arched. "I think Tony enjoys retirement for all of us. Let me run out and get some sweets to go along with tea. I am sure Tony will not object." She disappeared.

"Listen to this," Tony said. "They are reporting that NASA is sending some robots to the moon to look for water. What will they think of next?" He laughed.

"Tony, listen to me. I have an idea. I have never been a bureaucrat. Those NGOs spend too much time on budgets and proposals. It reminds me of the conversation we had a few years ago — about creating our own foundation."

I paused, waiting for Tony to jump in, but his eyes had wandered back to the TV.

I heard Scott Hubbard, the moon mission manager, say, "You won't see a lunar lake with moon penguins skating around on it."

"Tony, please turn that off. I want to talk to you."

He muted the sound and turned to me, keeping one eye on the screen. "Go ahead, but I'm not giving up my morning swims or my afternoon naps."

"Tony, our work isn't done. We both know too many children still go without the most basic education. Life isn't getting easier out there. Now there's prostitution, gangs, and drugs. We can't abandon them. CNN can wait."

Tony rubbed his hands but stayed silent.

"Tony, we can help, we can still do something. We are not too old. I need you to help me figure this out. I don't have enough personal money to take care of my family and establish a foundation. But I bet you know how to." I was a small step away from pleading.

Tony directed his gaze beyond the patio sliding doors. I knew that look: I was losing him.

I charged ahead. I needed to convince him. For them, for me, desperate measures were called for.

"How would you feel if Kay had to walk the streets or Max dealt in drugs?"

Tony glared at me. I had touched a nerve.

"Leave my kids out of this. It's not about them: it's about you. You can't leave it alone."

I had just attacked my best friend. What was wrong with me?

In a tone I had never heard Tony use, he said, "Amporn, I hear you. You need at least 5 million or 10 million *baht* to even think about a foundation or else you don't have a chance. That's assuming volunteers give you their blood. I won't risk that kind of money. And I am not interested." The finality of his words reverberated through the living room.

Recomposing himself, his expression softened. "Amporn, you've done so much for Thai children. Enjoy retirement. You have to face it: it's time to rest. Enjoy your hobbies. You have some, don't you?"

I heard a mix of pity and wishful thinking in his voice.

"How does one rejoice in the time of *tom yum goong?* My country is falling to pieces. The *baht* keeps tumbling. This is one of the biggest economic crises in Asia, and it all started here in Thailand. Who knows how far the regional economy will fall. The *baht* cannot be shored up any more. The banks are in chaos. The government will have to unpeg the *baht* from the U.S. dollar and let it float. The economy can no longer artificially support its own currency. The people will suffer. Who, I ask you, will help the poor? The children are not responsible for the economic mess our country is in."

"No, they are not. But neither are you. You cannot save every Thai child in need."

I rebelled against his words. I may have not been able to save every child, but I could continue to save one child at a time. I wanted to curse him … and God.

"I cannot stand by and do nothing. This is my country. These children are a shadow of myself."

The inhumanity sickened me. Nothing had changed. The dangers multiplied and worsened. Was it worse to starve sheltered by a large concrete pipe discarded from road construction in the middle of Bangkok or by a tarp-covered hut next to the village dump? Were the dangers of malnutrition or HIV/AIDS worth calculating? *Damn you, God, for making me believe there was hope.*

"Have you heard the latest?" Tony asked.

"About what?"

"CCF."

My blood was a raging tsunami. "No."

"I heard the new administration let some people go. Apparently the local office is overstaffed." Tony rolled his eyes.

I fumed. *That is more important than what I am talking to you about? Office gossip?*

"I heard 13 people got the ax in December. Can you believe it? No warning, nothing. They just told them 'Thank you for your services.'" Tony shook his head.

I struggled. I wanted to yell at him, at myself, at God. My anger robbed me of my breath. What was the purpose of my life? What I had done was not enough; I was not finished.

Tony said, "Yes, they were compensated. Could they not have waited until after Christmas? Head office worries too much about the balance sheet and not enough about the street children. Poverty does not run on a business plan."

I managed to eke out, "Tony, please stop."

He shrugged, reached for the remote control, and turned the sound back on. Within seconds his face relaxed, his eyes widened, and CNN fully engrossed him.

In that moment I realized I was alone. My good friend left everything familiar to come to my country and help Thai families, first as a priest and then by leading CCF. I could not ask any more of him.

***

Everyday bred more economic turmoil. The government was in disarray while trying to shore up the *baht* and themselves. The have-nots were incapable of doing anything but watching with alarm. The haves were busy offshoring or safeguarding what they had. The few in between, middle-class like me, were meaningless. Once again, I found myself powerless.

I no longer offered my consulting services, as fewer had money to pay me. The ones who did, searched for ways to save their skins. I spent my energy dreaming up schemes to rescue children and families trashed by this economic crash, named by corrupt officials for Thailand's favorite soup, *tom yum goong*—spicy and sour. At night, unable to sleep, I stared at the sky lighted by Bangkok's elite—restaurants, fancy offices, and shopping malls—and switched between cursing them and my own cozy existence. Only the faces of my own children curbed the desire to attempt suicide again.

Sunee worried about further devaluation and inflation. She sensed my general lack of interest in living. She had nightmares of the thin shack in Surin swallowing up our family. I no longer read the *Bangkok Post*. My tea grew cold before I took the first sip. The two cars in our driveway embarrassed me. No, they tormented me. They reminded me of my middle-class status. My drawers were filled with business cards, a reminder of my uselessness. I had done good work; I knew that. But in the face of the crises, I also realized I had traveled a very short distance. Access to deep pockets eluded me, when foreign charitable agencies could access them.

CHAPTER TWENTY-FIVE

BANGKOK'S DOWNTOWN streets bustled with nervous energy. Round-the-clock traffic noise filled the air under a sky mocking the city dwellers' uncertainty. The country's precarious economy threatened to plunge the entire region into chaos.

A few days into January of 1998, I stepped into the Thai Farmers' Bank to complete the final formality of my retirement, cashing my pension check. I detected a sense of purpose in each person who passed by. Whether feigned or real, their earnestness triggered resentment. My mood soured further. After that day, every day would be the same for the rest of my life. Some may call it relaxing, reaping the rewards after a long career, spending endless days resting and enjoying life. I saw it differently. Eventually, I hoped to figure out what could possibly be so engaging that I would welcome my days of idleness.

My family, on the other hand, had anticipated this moment for a long time. They already had plans for how to spend my retirement money. The first step would be sharing a celebratory meal at a Sukiyaki restaurant that night. They rejoiced at the end of my career. How did one mark with happiness the period in which he officially became useless to society? I forced myself to feel gratitude. This career had provided for each of them. My children had made me proud. Piak and Toum shadowed each other, both graduating with bachelors' in business administration, from different universities. Noum chose a different path. From his industrial technology college studies, he unleashed his entrepreneurial spirit and created his own body repair and auto parts company. Tata, our youngest daughter, lived nearby. She had an artistic inclination and followed her passion by securing a degree in fashion design.

Sunee had mentioned more than once that she looked forward to more family time together. She meant all of us. Our family reunions now included three very inquisitive little minds, my grandchildren. We had nicknamed Miss Jittapa, the eldest at 3 years old, Beam. She had a 1 year old brother, Pongpol, whom we referred to as Benz. Their father, my second son, Ampol, lived with his wife on the perimeter of Bangkok. The children had a cousin, Nana, officially named Matina. Although spared the white hair, I now cherished my new title, *Bpuu*, Grandfather.

I saw my reflection in the cashier's window. Was that really me? Was I really 60 years old? Yes, I told myself. *But look on the bright side, you retired and most people must work until they reach 65.* CCF had been kind. They offered me a lump sum for my time, on top of the monthly pension I now received — very generous. Then why did I feel like the burglar that had stolen *Songkran*, our Thai traditional New Year?

The teller's voice interrupted my reverie. "Dr. Amporn, we cashed your check. What would you like us to do with the 5 million *baht*?"

"How much did you say?" I stopped breathing.

"Five million *baht*." There must be a mistake. I was expecting 3.5 million *baht*. Wearing a blank expression, I waited for him to realize his error.

"Dr. Amporn, the *baht* is in free fall. Today the exchange rate hovers around $1 U.S. to 57 *baht*. At today's exchange rate, your one check in the amount of $88,000 U.S. converts to 5 million *baht*."

"I'll take all of it. With me, that is. Can I do that?" My heart beat double time. I wore a huge grin.

"Yes, the money is yours, Dr. Amporn."

I skipped out of the bank and headed for Tony's.

***

"Slow down, Amporn, I can't follow what you're saying." Tony muted the volume on CNN.

"I am so happy, Tony. Relieved, actually. I was so worried I would fail."

"Amporn, please slow down. Tell me what happened. Did you win the lottery?"

"In a way, I did."

His eyes glistened. He gestured for me to sit down. I ignored him and paced, crisscrossing the space between him and his beloved television. Where should I begin? There was so much to do.

"I went to cash my first retirement check, the payout for retiring at 60 instead of 65. I forgot that the *baht* has been falling since the New Year."

"You forgot?" Tony asked. He shadowed me, trying to block my movement.

I walked over to the open patio door and shouted: "Thank you, God."

"Amporn, what is going on? You were not this excited when you were named CFF's director. This is the first time I've heard you talk to God." Tony laughed a deep, belly laugh.

"Tony, after they converted the dollars, I got 5 million *baht*! Can you believe my good fortune? I got 5 million *baht*! This is the answer, Tony, the solution."

"The answer to what? You're confusing me. Are you in financial trouble? Why didn't you tell me?"

"No, no. This is the answer to funding my own foundation. You will help too, won't you? My dream is becoming a reality. I will establish a new foundation. We will help the children, young and old. We can change things for so many. Don't you see?"

"Amporn, take a breath. Are you saying you want to spend your pension payout on creating a new charity?"

"It won't be all my retirement, only the part I negotiated with CCF for leaving five years early. I wanted to stay until 65. Anyway, that's behind me now. I agreed with them in the end. I told you I wanted to have my own foundation. But I didn't have the money. God works in mysterious ways. This is His will for me. I know it."

I stopped my to-and-fro and stood squarely in front of him.

He said, "You want to spend your retirement savings so you can work harder?"

"Yes."

"What do *Khun* Sunee and your children think about this?" Tony asked.

"They're against it. I have a right to do this. I worked hard all my life. I provided well for them. We live comfortably. They want for nothing. If we live frugally, the monthly pension is more than enough for us to live on. The lump-sum payout for those five years from 60 to 65 is mine. I get to choose what I do with it and this is what I want: to set up my own Thai foundation to help Thai children."

"Amporn, you should think this over. Give your family the time to come around to the idea. Their support matters. As for me, I—"

I cut him off. The words rushed from my mouth like water over a dam. "Tony, I have made up my mind, with or without your blessing, I am going to do it. It is nonnegotiable. We require an office, staff, and many volunteers. I want this to be a proper organization. Who will guide me? The executive committee should be composed of people willing to put their names and reputations on the line. This will give the foundation credibility and help with fund-raising. I want people who believe in making a difference. I will avoid those who lust for prestige. We need a name. Maybe you have ideas. Words come easily to you. There will be lots of paperwork, tasks, projects ..."

The urgency of tackling this new project energized me. I nodded to Tony and headed out the door, convinced I had made the right decision.

For once, words failed him.

***

For the next three weeks, adrenaline fueled me. I secured office space in the Suan Luang district of Bangkok. Still somewhat superstitious, I saw a good omen when I discovered the famous Mae Nak Shrine once occupied the space we leased. The famous shrine, which recently moved to another address in the same district, honored Lady Nak, a well-known Thai ghost. She figured at the center of a love story in which a mother died during childbirth while her husband served in the army far away. He returned, unaware that his wife had refused to move into her afterlife. He learned of her fate when she appeared to him in the guise of a human. A venerable monk came to his aid, captured Lady Nak, and confined her spirit. Although many versions of the tale abound, few contested the undying devotion Lady Nak offered to her husband. For once, a ghost who nurtured love accompanied me.

***

My foundation occupied the ground floor of an eight-story apartment building. The buzz of activity spilled onto the street. We discussed our agenda in a freshly painted space filled with bookshelves, tables, computers, a telephone/fax line — and unbridled energy.

Everyone had a mobile phone. Bangkok had long tentacles that entangled staff in traffic, meetings in opposite ends of the city, and bureaucratic labyrinths. The phones eased the burden of communicating. We installed air conditioning and additional lighting for workdays that extended long past sundown. I deposited 200,000 *baht* in the bank, a guarantee for our operating expenses. So far, the bills totaled 1 million *baht*. Sometimes, the magnitude of those obligations triggered fear within me. Money evaporated while our list of needs grew faster than wild bamboo. Once initiated, the programs would burn through the money even faster.

The space may have been as cramped as an ant colony, but the brightness of everyone's hopes and goals created a rich atmosphere. I loved everything about being there. People came and went from morning until dark. They worked with purposeful enthusiasm on their specific tasks. We were a large family rooting for our favorite team. We did not know the meaning of dissent.

One day, I overheard part of a conversation: "I love this. It reminds me of the early days of Laurel and Hardy at CCF." A direct reference to Tony and me. Thinking of him left a small pang of longing. Yet, the lightness in my soul nearly lifted me off the ground. We paid rent for three months, which I thought would be should be long enough to launch our mission.

I hired my previous CFF employees who had been laid off. Nit Taramongkol moved over as accountant and finance manager. Julie Jarusvichakorn was the administrative assistant. Suzie Sae-Ton was the office manager. At first, I hesitated to hire Jukkrit

Panruangsakao as head of fund-raising. After reconsideration, I realized handling fund-raising by myself would be too much. He hired Dang Pattama to be his assistant. Jukkrit and Dang faced the greatest challenge of all. They commanded the highest salaries. Keeping them would depend on their own success of raising money. Everyone agreed to a significant salary cut. They appreciated any work during Thailand's economic plunge. I wished I could have paid them more. They deserved it. But it remained outside my reach — at least at that time.

I arrived in the early morning hours, before everyone else. I enjoyed this moment of calm, sipping my tea, looking forward to the day's progress. I breathed in the tranquility. When it became hectic later in the day, I would drink from this reservoir. Each time I signed a check or made another decision, my stomach contracted. I reminded myself that Mother Mary looked after me. I thrived, emboldened by the rightness of our mission. She knew that. She would not fail me. I was convinced that she had guided me here to fulfill my life's purpose.

Julie walked into my office. "*Sawadee.* Good morning, Dr. Amporn."

Her bangs framed dark eyes filled with childlike joy, which belied her fierce determination. She may have been petite in stature, but she was a tsunami of dedication. Over time, I knew I would need to teach her how to harness her own power. For the moment, I watched, with gratitude and appreciation, whenever she unleashed it.

She giggled with youthful enthusiasm. "What monkey are we wrestling today?"

She had single-handedly purchased our desks at a discount, convinced the local print shop to charge us for 500 copies while providing 1,000, and cajoled the postal carriers into taking two parcels for the price of one.

"*Sawadee, Khun* Julie, I have good news. I found our fourth director. Including myself, we now have the five members required to register the foundation. We have an alumnus from my MBA program, *Khun* Cholatarn; Dr. Sunthorn, the local radio announcer; *Khun* Than-yawan; and my son, Ampol. Today we must work very hard to find a name for our foundation, the one missing piece."

"Let's do it, then."

Well past nine in the evening, I was alone in the office. I forced the others to leave earlier because most commuted long distances. I surveyed the empty teacups scattered on the desks, the crumpled food wrappers, the scribbled notes taped to the wall under various headings: Children, Help, Education, Growth, Needy, Survive, Alone, Together, Read, Write, Family, School, Future, Helping Hands, Tomorrow, Give. Our creative powers had not risen to the occasion. We had yet to find a name for the foundation that resonated with the entire group. During the course of the day, our collective energy had morphed into frustration. Jukkrit and Dang became impatient. Fund-raising was far more important to them. They would have traded in all this wordplay to get back to their task.

***

"We can't let our difficulty choosing a name dampen our spirits. Morale has bottomed out. Why?"

"You push us too hard, Dr. Amporn. There is no perfect name." Julie spoke softly, almost reverentially. This tentativeness was contrary to her usual demeanor.

"We want to file tomorrow. But none of the names satisfy you. Our work accumulates, yet for three days this is all we have concentrated on." Irritation crept into her voice. "Is it that important?" Julie glanced up at me.

Why did I feel so indecisive about the name? Mine changed several times. By naming the foundation, we were baptizing it and bringing it forth into the community. Was I losing my courage?

Closing my eyes, I whispered to myself: "Mary, Mother, please help me. Please give me strength to move forward." Heaving a sigh, I headed to the wall, where I taped a fresh piece of paper. In thick, blue letters I wrote: FOUNDATION FOR THE REHABILITATION AND DEVELOPMENT OF CHILDREN.

Everyone spontaneously applauded. We had it.

"*Khun* Julie, how long will the registration process take?" I asked.

"They told me about six months," she said.

"Oh!"

I wished Julie had informed me sooner that it would take so long to process the paperwork. I had wanted everything to work to my timetable. It may have sounded silly, but I had wanted the foundation to be born in February, the month of love. I had wanted it to be a Valentine's baby. Gloom overtook me. Here it was again. The step back.

***

A few days later, I left the Bangkok Marriott Hotel after a conference on the education and overall welfare of Thai children. Although I was technically retired and without a title, they, nonetheless, HAD invited me. The discussions should have held my attention, but they seemed distant to me — too formal and heavy on theory.

I walked out of the hotel, eager to get back to the office and to my action plan.

"*Khun* Amporn?" I heard my name and turned around.

"*Khun* Chantamol," I said, recognizing an old acquaintance. We had met in 1995 at a Pre-Olympic Games conference organized by Jimmy Carter.

"What brings you here?" I asked.

"It's been a long time since Atlanta, *Khun* Amporn. I am now director general for the Cultural Division of the Ministry of Education. My colleagues and I were attending the meetings. How about you? What keeps you busy these days?"

"I've retired, a doctor," I blurted out in a not-so-subtle attempt to impress him.

He appeared confused.

"I was awarded an honorary degree."

"Good for you." He bowed in a *wei* of respect.

I seized the opportunity. "But retirement is overrated." I smiled intentionally. "I am now creating my own foundation to help homeless children receive a basic education."

"I see."

"But we are having some early problems. We are caught in a paperwork nightmare, waiting for the registration to come through. It takes so long. My hands are tied until we receive the official papers. I—"

Khun Chantamol's cell phone rang. He gestured for me to wait. "I must go, *Khun*, ah, Dr. Amporn."

"Let me look into it, for old times' sake. I have a few connections." With that, he disappeared into the crowd of suits.

***

The Foundation For The Rehabilitation And Development Of Children was officially founded on February 14, 1998. Valentine's Day is considered the most auspicious day on which to register one's marriage. Thai people believe that marriages sealed on this day last forever. It was not a coincidence that FORDEC was born on this day.

CHAPTER TWENTY-SIX

I FELT overwhelmed by all that I wanted to do and all that I needed to do. My staff's enthusiasm coursed through my veins, infusing me with a feeling of invulnerability. Everything was possible now that I had my own foundation. Wherever I looked, the streets of Bangkok swelled with children in need of assistance. I saw an all too familiar look in their eyes — and it made me shudder.

We named our first program "Education and Development for Poor Students." The idea was simple. We would sponsor children to attend a local school by providing one basic meal per day and money for school supplies and uniforms. Julie ushered one child after another into our offices. They all needed help: boys and girls; shy, small, disheveled children, all unsure of why they existed.

"Dr. Amporn, this is Piyarat. Her mother brought her to us because she heard we might help her go to school." Hiding behind Julie's skirt, the wide-eyed little girl poked her head out. Her dark eyes darted from the typewriters, to the desks and chalkboard. She tugged at Julie's skirt and whispered something.

"She wants to know," Julie said, "if she goes to school, could she work here someday. She says it is too smelly and dirty where her mother works."

All I could see of the little girl were her eyes, the color of dark, teak wood. I realized it was not so much a question as a demand for a promise. She tugged at Julie's skirt again.

"She wants to know if her baby sister can study with her. She is the same age. When she brought them here, her mother told me they are twins. She picks through trash and sells what she can to feed her daughters." Piyarat pulled Julie's hand once more. She did not say anything, just looked up at her. Then, in an unabashed way, she looked me straight the eye. Her gaze was intense, almost fierce. Her face softened and she nodded enough to hold my attention. I nodded back. She grabbed Julie's hand and pulled her out of the office. I had agreed to sponsor yet another child.

***

"Tony, I can't thank you and *Khun* Dusanee enough for sponsoring Piyarat and her sister. That little girl has a fighting spirit in her. Without you, I would have had to turn them down. I'm already out of money, I don't know what I am going to do."

"Amporn, we are happy to help. You know that. These girls deserve a basic education. But what are you going to do? It's only been a few months since you started."

I collapsed on the couch in Tony's living room. My visits had become more infrequent as my troubles mounted. We had carefully controlled our expenses as we set up FORDEC. Once we launched our programs, I began to lose control, finding myself incapable of saying no.

Each mother and father that brought us their child wore the same mask of supplication. They did everything they could to survive. Nothing more could be asked of them. But it was not enough. Their son or daughter represented their only hope. They were powerless. I was not. So, I would say yes to this child until I found more funding. But my pension funds had run dry, and no other sponsors had been found.

"Hey Tony, did I tell you that *Thai Praew* ran an article on July 25, 1999 about my life story and how FORDEC was created?"

"Amporn, do not change the subject. This is not like the old days. There is no head office to save you. You have committed to all these people and you are running out of money. I am concerned. You can't keep using your personal funds. What will happen to your own family?"

"That's my problem, not yours. Good day, Tony. Thank you for your help. Please tell *Khun* Dusanee thank you for sponsoring the two girls. Enjoy your swim." I left before he could stop me.

***

The nights became shorter and the days longer. I resented the very comfort of my house and my own bed. The few hours I slept were interrupted by nightmares. Darkness plunged me back onto the streets of Surin. Over and over, I saw those noodles ground into the dirt by fat, wealthy, well-dressed men who laughed at me. Or, I would see the faces of the Bangkok elite frowning with disgust or wagging their index fingers at me. Once in a while, Father Masterson or Father Bonningue would appear, silent, observing me. I hated those apparitions more than the nightmares. It reminded me that I was failing where they had succeeded. They had backed the wrong man.

I lost my appetite and spent more hours in the office. I insisted that Nit prepare a daily report of our current financial situation. The picture was bleak. Julie had stopped bringing in new children.

For a few weeks, we were distracted by our commitment to help the Chanukroh Elderly and Child Care Center. The owner had approached us for funding. That was out of the question for the moment. Their facilities were in such a state of disrepair that we spent a few days repairing their buildings, bathrooms and playground. It helped morale among the staff. But it plunged me further into despair.

I even stopped praying to the Virgin Mary. At one time, she may have loved me as her son, but I was failing. More often, I found myself sitting in the dark, intentionally replaying bad memories from my past. The more painful or ugly they were, the better. I was reviving the old Lek, the one who came back from the jungle. I delved into those hours of misery back in Surin that led me to my first suicide attempt and then my second. But I would not let myself remember the kindness of the Thai woman who had saved me. Instead, I reminded myself that I had not outmaneuvered my past. I had simply outrun it for a while. But now it was back to claim me. I was a failure.

Depression set in. I went to the office less often. I left it to Julie to make decisions. I became weak. My family decided that I must be sick as they had never seen me like this before. On August 23, 1999, they admitted me to Vejthani Hospital. My body was not sick; my spirit was. For the third time in my life, suicide seemed like the only solution. I did not tell anyone what I was contemplating. I simply reverted to being Lek, alone and vulnerable.

***

"Dr. Amporn, this is Julie. I know you are at the hospital. I asked the doctor, and he said you were well enough to speak to me. I am sorry I have not visited. I've been very busy with all our programs."

"Hello, *Khun* Julie. It is fine. You need not visit me." I cut her off.

"Dr. Amporn, I do not know how to say this. We have received a call from the managing director of the Export-Import Bank. He insists on meeting with you tomorrow, August 24. I, I think, he may be considering a donation. He would not say. But he was insistent on meeting you for lunch tomorrow. What shall …"

I did not hear the nurse come into my room. At the same moment Julie was explaining the reason for her call, the nurse took my hand to check my hospital bracelet. Her touch was soft but firm. I looked up at the nurse but I did not see her. I saw the Thai woman from when I was 17, lying in the hospital in Surin. I heard her voice. "Lek, you're too young to give up."

"*Khun* Julie, tell the director I'll be there. I will meet him for lunch tomorrow."

***

I returned to work the following week. Actually, I returned to being Amporn. I still do not know why I became so discouraged, why I lost hope at the beginning of FORDEC's second year. The man from the Export-Import Bank, on behalf of himself and his wife, made a generous contribution over lunch. That seed donation from a stranger made it possible for me to take a step back, evaluate where we were, and set a sound course for the future of FORDEC. After all, I was only 62; I was still young. Besides, Piyarat and I had an understanding that, when she graduated, she would come to work for FORDEC. I would need her. I planned that someday FORDEC would create its own daycare center — a place where lost children could find their way.

FOUNDATION FOR REHABILITATION AND DEVELOPMENT OF CHILDREN AND FAMILY (FORDEC)

FORDEC is a nonprofit, charitable organization dedicated to creating hope for Thai children and their families, regardless of gender, race, or religion, who suffer from the effects of poverty. FORDEC helps them with basic needs such as food, health care, and education.

If you are interested in making a donation, sponsoring a child, or would like more information about FORDEC, please consult their website at http://fordecthai.org/ and follow them on Facebook.

GLOSSARY

Thai words and expressions can be translated in various ways. I have chosen the transliteration most familiar to Dr. Amporn. My sole intention is to assist the reader with a general understanding of the usage. These are by no means full explanations.

baht: Thai currency. On July 24, 2014, 1 *baht* = .0314 U.S. dollar (or approximately 30 *baht* to $1 U.S.).

Bikkhu: Ordained Buddhist male monk.

bodhi: Sacred fig tree under which Buddha achieved enlightenment. Bodhi trees are planted close to Buddhist monasteries.

bugambilias: bougainvillea. Vine-growing plant with showy purple, pink, orange, or scarlet flowers.

Bodhisath (also, *Bodhisattva*): The Buddha in his former lives. Also refers to someone motivated by great compassion.

Bpuu: Grandfather. Term used to refer to a paternal grandfather.

chut tai: Traditional Thai attire. For men, this usually includes pants and a Nehru-style jacket or shirt.

Dharma: A Buddhist term having many meanings but used here mainly to refer to either the natural way of things, universal law, or the Buddhist teachings referring to Enlightenment and the Path to realize it.

durian: Fruit encased in an odorific, thorny husk.

farang: Foreign, foreigner(s).

galangal: A plant in the ginger family used in Thai cooking. Similar in flavor to plain ginger, but stronger in taste.

graab: Five-point prostration.

Hah Taew: Five Sacred Lines.

Jatakas: Tales concerning the previous lives of the Buddha, which often exemplify universal virtues and truths.

jivorn: Outer robe, usually of saffron color, worn by Thai Buddhist monks.

jok: Rice porridge or congee. Often eaten as a meal when combined with other ingredients.

kalamona: Hardwood tree with brilliant yellow, cascading flowers.

Kammuang: Language that resembles Thai and Lao, spoken in northern Thailand.

ka: A part of speech indicating politeness, used in the Thai language. Often used to indicate the end of a statement.

kap: A polite way to answer "yes" to a question. Sometimes it is used by itself to indicate that the listener is still paying attention.

khanom pia: Chinese-type dessert with a dough-like crust, usually filled with beans. Other ingredients may be added to make it savory, salty, or sweet.

Khun: A commonly used address before the first name of men and women, intended as a show of respect.

klong: Canal in central Thailand used for transportation and drainage.

Kob kun krap: "Thank you," spoken by a man.

kutti: Small and simple cottage where monks sleep, often on or near temple grounds.

Luang Phu: Respected Grandfather, a title conferred upon a respected senior Buddhist monk old enough to be the monk's grandfather.

Luang Por: Venerable Father, a title conferred upon respected senior Buddhist monks.

Luang Ta: Venerable Uncle, a title conferred upon senior Buddhist monks without titles.

Maha: Great. In this context, refers to a title granted to a monk who has reached a certain high level in *Pali* studies.

muay Thai: A combat sport, also known as Thai kickboxing.

mudra: Position of the body, sometimes only of hand or fingers, intended to have symbolic meaning or to influence the energies or moods of the body.

naga: Clever snake. In Buddhist legend, a *naga* disguised itself as a man in order to be ordained as a monk.

nam pla: Dark fish sauce common in Southeast Asian cuisine.

nat: Banyan tree or leaves.

neem: (leaves) Sometimes referred to as *sadow* leaf. It is an evergreen tree with white flowers. In traditional medicine, its leaves are used (among other uses) to combat malaria, provide dental hygiene, and treat urinary tract problems.

Nehn: Novice monk in Thailand.

Nong: Younger person, often used to refer to a brother or sister.

nora: Performance tradition of dance, drama, and ritual in some south Thailand villages.

Pali: Line or canonical text. Language of original Buddhist scriptures, still chanted in rituals.

pansa: Rainy season in Thailand.

Phra: Normal title for monks in Thailand.

prang: Elongated tower or spire characteristic of Thai temple architecture.

rambutan: Tropical fruit, similar to lychee.

sabong: Monk's under robe, usually worn around the waist, covering the belly button and extending to just below the knees.

sala: Open pavilion used as a meeting place, inside or outside temple grounds.

Sangha: Buddhist community of ordained monks.

sawadee: Greeting, "Hello."

Songkran: Traditional Thai New Year's festival celebrated April 13–15.

sowai: Beautiful.

suat: Chanting, as a component of Buddhist ceremonies.

sutra: Recitation of oral precepts, in this case

during a funeral, in hope of making merit to be transmitted to the departed.

tom yum goong: Thai hot and sour soup. Also refers to the 1997 financial crisis in Asia which began in Thailand.

ungsa: Under robe worn by monks, typically, a thin undershirt.

Waan Jai: Sweetheart

wat: Sacred compound of a Buddhist temple; sometimes, also includes monks' quarters and a school.

wei: (noun and verb) Thai greeting of respect: a slight bow with palms pressed together at chest level. Also, indicates gratitude or an apology.

Wheel of Dharma: The chief symbol of Buddhism, usually consists of a chariot wheel with different numbers of spokes. The hub, rim, and spokes represent dharma, mindfulness, and moral discipline.

ACKNOWLEDGMENTS

First and foremost, I wish to express my deep gratitude to Dr. Amporn Wathanavongs for the privilege of writing his life story. It is an act of courage to bare one's soul and entrust one's story to another to tell. His patience over the years, throughout many long interviews and his explanations of Thai culture, especially his years within the robes, were invaluable. With good humor he supported my efforts every step of the way, including numerous revisions. I am eternally grateful for his life, for the gift of knowing him, and for his unending support.

I am deeply grateful to my husband, Bill Thomas, for his boundless encouragement. Without him, I would not have met Dr. Amporn, nor had the opportunity to write his extraordinary life story. Without Bill cheering me on, I might have put down my pen early and often. His love and unending support was the one constant that guided me through the many years of this project.

My gratitude goes to the staff of FORDEC, who kindly sent me information and photos and traveled with me to the Thai countryside. Special thanks go to Julie Sumalee Jarusvichakorn and all the children of *Wat Mahawong* Community Day Care Center FORDEC 6. Their smiles, songs, and unabashed *joie de vivre* inspired me. I wish to acknowledge Dusanee Tersch and her late husband Tony Tersch for their unwavering support. Peter Robinson offered valuable insights into Buddhism and the practices of novices and monks in Thailand, and provided other valuable commentary.

As a first-time author, I am indebted to many people who mentored me, inspired me, and critiqued my work: to the members of the North Street Writers Group, especially Mary Scherf and Gerry Lantz for their generous commentaries; and to Beth Rubin who edited my work with such commitment and dedication, offering fresh insights, direct critique, and needed faith in my work. And to the many others, such as Audra O'Brien, too numerous to name.

I want to express my appreciation to my mother, who has steadfastly encouraged me as I have launched into a new career as a writer. And to my friend Janet Bernstein, one of my greatest allies.

Lastly, I am profoundly in John Mooney's debt, for the valuable role he has played to bring this book to publication. I am grateful for his thoughtful insights, generosity of efforts and openness to my suggestions as we crafted this book. His conviction that this story had to be told is every writer's dream. Thank you.